DASH DIET COOKBOOK FOR BEGINNERS

Quick, Healthy & Delicious Low Sodium Recipes To Lose Weight, Reduce Blood Pressure,Boost Metabolism, & Embrace a Natural Diet

6 WEEKS MEAL PLAN

EMILY WACHOB

TABLE OF CONTENT

INTRODUCTION

WHAT IS DASH DIET?

The DASH diet is an acronym for specific Dietary Approach to Stop Hypertension. The diet was developed to help people lower their blood pressure without medication. The idea behind the diet is to minimize sodium in your diet and eat more foods that are high in potassium, calcium, and magnesium. These nutrients are known as electrolytes, and they help to regulate blood pressure. The DASH diet also includes plenty of fruits, vegetables, whole grains, and low-fat dairy products. The main goal is to add a variety of healthy foods to your diet that will provide your body with all the essential nutrients needed to function properly. While the DASH diet is not specifically a weight loss diet, eating healthy foods can help you maintain a healthy weight, which is important for overall health.

Why Choose The Dash Diet?

The dash diet is a popular choice for those looking to improve their health. And it's no wonder- the dash diet has been shown in terms of lowering blood pressure, improve cholesterol levels, as well as reduce the risk of heart disease and stroke. But that's not all- the dash diet can also help you, fight diabetes and even boost your energy levels. If you want to improve your physical and mental health, then the dash diet is a great place to start. Here are some reasons why the dash diet is a good choice:

It's rich in nutrient-dense foods

The dash diet emphasizes on eating plenty of vegetables, fruits, vegetables, and low-fat dairy. This ensures that you are getting all the essential nutrients your body needs.

It helps lower blood pressure

Some studies have shown that the dash diet can help to lower blood pressure, even in people who don't have hypertension.

It reduces the risk of heart disease

The dash diet has been shown quite effective to reduce the prominent risk of developing heart disease, making it a good choice for those with a family history of heart problems.

It aids weight loss

Because it's rich in fruits, vegetables, and whole grains, the dash diet can help you lose extra weight in a healthy way.

It lowers cholesterol

The dash diet helps to lower LDL (bad) cholesterol and raise HDL (good) cholesterol, which can reduce your risk of developing cardiovascular diseases.

It helps prevent diabetes

By helping you lose weight and keeping blood sugar levels under control, the dash diet can also help to prevent type 2 diabetes.

It's easy to follow

Unlike some other diets, the dash diet is easy to adapt and stick to long-term because it doesn't eliminate any food groups or require special foods.

It's flexible

You can tailor the dash diet to your own individual needs and preferences, making it easy to fit into your lifestyle.

It's affordable

There is no need to spend in terms of spending lots of money on special foods or supplements to follow the dash diet - just eat plenty of fresh fruits, vegetables and whole grains.

It's delicious

Last but not least, the dash diet is also delicious! You'll enjoy eating plenty of healthy and tasty foods while following this plan.

TIPS FOR DASH DIET

The DASH diet is a complete and lifelong approach to healthy eating that is developed to help treat or prevent high blood pressure, heart disease, and stroke. The DASH diet encourages to reduce intake of sodium in your diet along with eating a variety of foods that are high in nutrients that lower blood pressure, such as potassium, calcium, and magnesium. As part of the DASH diet, you're also encouraged to increase your daily consumption of fruits, vegetables, whole grains, and low-fat or nonfat dairy products and limit your intake of saturated fats, red meats, sweets, and sugary drinks. In addition to making dietary changes, the DASH diet also recommends that you get at least 30 minutes of moderate-intensity physical activity—such as walking—most days of the week. Here are some useful tips that can help you make the DASH diet a success:

Fill up on fruits and vegetables

The DASH diet includes lots of colorful fruits as well as vegetables as part of a healthy eating plan. These foods are packed with nutrients that help to lower blood pressure, like potassium, calcium, and magnesium.

Go for low-fat or fat-free dairy products

To satisfy your hunger without increasing your saturated fat intake, choose low-fat or fat-free dairy products. The DASH diet includes milk, yogurt, cheese, and other dairy products as part of a healthy eating plan.

Add protein-rich foods to meals and snacks That Satisfy Hunger

To keep from getting too hungry between meals, add protein-rich foods such as lean meat, fish, poultry, beans, tofu, nuts, and seeds to meals and snacks throughout the day.

Satisfy Your Sweet Tooth Cravings in A Healthy Way

The DASH diet doesn't ban sweets altogether, but it does recommend limiting sugary desserts, such as cake, cookies, and candy. To satisfy all your cravings in a healthy way, try incorporating fruit into your dessert or snack instead.

Drink Plenty Of Fluids

Most people need about 2 liters (8 cups) of fluid a day.. While water is always a good choice, other beverages can also be helpful, such as unsweetened tea, coffee (without added sugar) or seltzer water. Just be sure to limit fluids that contain caffeine or alcohol, which can actually increase blood pressure.

Shop Smart

When you're at the grocery store, look for foods that are low in sodium as well as unhealthy fats. You can also check food labels to see how much sodium is in a product before you buy it. Look for articles on the dash diet for more ideas about what to buy at the grocery store.

Limit Eating Out

When you're dining out, it can be challenging to find foods that fit into the dash diet. Many restaurants serve large portions of food that are high in sodium. If you do eat out, try to find restaurants that offer healthier options or give you the option to customize your order.

Address Emotional Eating

Some people turn to food when they're feeling anxious, stressed out or depressed. If emotional eating is a problem for you, there are practices you can adapt to address it head on. Talk to your doctor or a therapist about how best to manage these feelings so they don't lead to unhealthy eating habits.

Get Moving

The best practice to improve your health is to get active, and that's one of the key components of the DASH diet. Aim for an at least 30 minutes of moderate exercise on some days of the week. Walking is a great way to get going.

Consult Your Doctor

Talk to your doctor or a Registered Dietitian Nutritionist if you have questions about whether the DASH diet is right for you or how to implement it into your own eating plan.

These 10 tips will set you up for success in following the dash diet long term. By following these tips you'll not only improve your eating habits but also your overall health.

RECOMMENDED FOODS

The DASH diet is a developed eating pattern that is recommended by the National Heart, Lung, and Blood Institute to help prevent and manage hypertension, or high blood pressure. The diet is full of vegetables, fruits, whole grains, and low-fat dairy foods, and it limits salt, red meat, sweets, and sugary beverages. While there are no such specific foods that are required on the DASH diet, there are certain food groups that are emphasized. These include:

Fruits

Aim for 4-5 servings per day. Choose fresh, frozen, or canned fruits (with no added sugar), 100% fruit juice, or dried fruit.

Vegetables

Eat 4-5 servings of vegetables per day. Include a variety of fresh, frozen, or even canned vegetables (with no added salt), and aim for at least one dark green and one orange vegetable per day.

Grains

6-8 servings per day. Choose whole grains such as oatmeal, whole wheat bread, brown rice, quinoa, barley, or popcorn. Limit refined grains such as white bread or pasta.

Protein

2-3 servings per day. Include lean meats such as chicken or turkey breast (without the skin), fish, shellfish, beans (legumes), eggs, nuts and seeds. Limit red meat and processed meats such as bacon or sausage.

Dairy

2-3 servings per day. Consume low-fat or fat-free milk, yogurt and cheese. If you are vegan or lactose intolerant, you can get your calcium from fortified plant milks, tofu, kale, broccoli, or almonds.

Salt

Limit sodium to 2,300 mg per day (about 1 tsp). This includes sodium from all sources - not just the salt shaker! Processed foods often contain hidden salt - check nutrition labels to see how much sodium is in a serving of food. If you have hypertension, your doctor may recommend a lower sodium intake - talk to your doctor about what is right for you.

Sugary beverages

Limit sugary drinks to no more than 36 ounces (450 ml) per week .This includes soda, fruit juice, sports drinks, and sweetened iced tea.

Alcohol

If you choose to consume alcohol, be moderate. For healthy adults, one drink per day, whereas for women of all ages and men over age 65, and up to two drinks per day for men 65 and younger.

Other considerations

If you have diabetes, you might want to be careful about monitoring your carbohydrate intake. Speak with your doctor or registered dietitian nutritionist about what is right for you. If you are following the DASH diet, you may need to limit potassium rich foods such as bananas, avocados, potatoes and tomatoes. Check and consult with your doctor before making any abrupt changes to your diet.

FOODS TO AVOID

Are you thinking of starting the DASH diet? If so, congratulations! The DASH diet is a proven way to lower blood pressure and improve overall health. However, as with any diet, there are certain foods that should be avoided. Here are some foods anyone adapting the DASH diet must avoid

Sodium-rich processed foods

Processed meats, canned soups and frozen dinners are high in sodium and must be avoided on the DASH diet. Instead, opt for fresh or frozen fruits and vegetables, lean protein sources, and whole grains.

Sugary drinks

Sodas, fruit juices and iced teas are full of sugar and empty calories. Stick to water or unsweetened tea instead.

Sweets

Cakes, cookies and other sweet treats are loaded with sugar and unhealthy fats. If you have a sweet tooth craving, try to satisfy it with fresh fruit or a small square of dark chocolate.
By following these tips, you'll be well on your way to success on the DASH diet!

FREQUENTLY ASKED QUESTIONS

The DASH diet is a popular and effective eating plan that has been shown to help in lowering and maintaining a normal blood pressure and improve heart health. While the diet is relatively straightforward, there are still a few questions that people often have about it. Some frequently asked questions about the dash diet are:

What can I eat on the dash diet?

The DASH diet emphasizes fruits, vegetables, whole grains, and low-fat dairy. It also limits salt, saturated fat, and added sugars.

What are the prominent advantages of the dash diet?

The DASH diet has been effective in terms of lowering blood pressure and improve heart health. It may also help to minimize the risk of stroke and other cardiovascular diseases.

How long do I need to follow the dash diet? You can follow the dash diet for as long as you like. However, if you're looking to see results, experts recommend following the plan for at least two weeks.

Can I cheat on the dash diet?

There's no need to cheat on the dash diet! Just make sure that you're getting plenty of fruits, vegetables, whole grains, and low-fat dairy. And limit your intake of salt, saturated fat and added sugars.

Following these simple guidelines will help you reap all the specific benefits of the dash diet!

Scroll to the end and **SCAN** the

QR CODE to download your **GIFT**

BREAKFAST RECIPES

EGG VEGETARIAN BREAKFAST SALAD

Easy

12 minutes

4 Servings

INGREDIENTS:

- 4 tablespoons lemon juice
- 6 teaspoons olive oil
- 2 cups avocado
- ½ teaspoon sea salt
- 3 cups grape tomatoes
- 1 cup red onion
- ½ teaspoon black pepper
- 6 cups organic arugula
- 8 large eggs, free range

PREPARATION:

1. Take a bowl and add oil and lemon juice.
2. Combine well and top with avocado, followed by onion, tomatoes, and arugula.
3. Refrigerate overnight and then dust with salt and black pepper.
4. Add this mixture in a pan and cook on medium-low heat for 5 minutes.
5. Add the eggs on top of the salad and dish out to serve.

NUTRITIONAL INFORMATION PER SERVING:

Calories	400
	% Daily Value*
Total Fat 31.8g	41%
Saturated Fat 7.3g	36%
Cholesterol 372mg	124%
Sodium 397mg	17%
Total Carbohydrate 16.6g	6%
Dietary Fiber 7.7g	28%
Total Sugars 6.9g	
Protein 16.4g	
Vitamin D 35mcg	175%
Calcium 132mg	10%
Iron 3mg	18%
Potassium 983mg	21%

STEEL-CUT OATS

Very Easy

6 minutes

4 Servings

INGREDIENTS:

- 3 cups water
- 1 cup steel-cut oats
- 2 cinnamon sticks

PREPARATION:

1. Merge the oats, water, and cinnamon sticks in a pressure cooker.
2. Fasten the lid and pressure cook for 6 minutes.
3. Do the quick pressure release and eliminate the cinnamon sticks.
4. Stir the oats well and dish out to serve.

NUTRITIONAL INFORMATION PER SERVING:

Calories	264
	% Daily Value*
Total Fat 4.2g	5%
Saturated Fat 0.8g	4%
Cholesterol 0mg	0%
Sodium 8mg	0%
Total Carbohydrate 45.6g	17%
Dietary Fiber 7.1g	25%
Total Sugars 0g	
Protein 10g	
Vitamin D 0mcg	0%
Calcium 16mg	1%
Iron 0mg	0%
Potassium 6mg	0%

SUMMER SKILLET VEGETABLE AND EGG

Very Easy

1 minute & 30 Seconds

4 Servings

INGREDIENTS:

- 12 ounces baby potatoes, thinly sliced
- 2 tablespoons olive oil
- 1¼ cups mushrooms, thinly sliced
- 1¼ cups zucchini
- ½ teaspoon rosemary
- 6 large eggs, lightly beaten
- ½ teaspoon salt
- 1¼ cups bell peppers
- 3 scallions, thinly sliced, green and white parts separated
- ½ teaspoon thyme
- 2 cups baby spinach

PREPARATION:

1. In a cast-iron skillet, put olive oil and potatoes and cook for about 8 minutes, constantly stirring.
2. Add bell peppers, zucchini, mushrooms, and scallion whites.
3. Cook for about 10 minutes, stirring occasionally, until golden brown in color.
4. Stir in the herbs and move the vegetables to the side of the pan.
5. Switch the heat to medium-low and whisk in the eggs with scallion greens.
6. Scramble softly for about 2 minutes and add baby spinach.
7. Eliminate from the heat and dust with salt before serving.

NUTRITIONAL INFORMATION PER SERVING:

Calories	247
	% Daily Value*
Total Fat 14.9g	19%
Saturated Fat 3.4g	17%
Cholesterol 279mg	93%
Sodium 424mg	18%
Total Carbohydrate 17.4g	6%
Dietary Fiber 4g	14%
Total Sugars 3.8g	
Protein 13.8g	
Vitamin D 105mcg	525%
Calcium 101mg	8%
Iron 6mg	32%
Potassium 801mg	17%

BERRY-ALMOND SMOOTHIE BOWL

Very Easy

10 minutes

2 Servings

INGREDIENTS:

- ½ cup frozen sliced banana
- ⅔ cup frozen raspberries
- ½ cup plain almond milk, unsweetened
- ¼ teaspoon ground cinnamon
- ⅛ teaspoon vanilla extract
- 1 tablespoon coconut flakes, unsweetened
- 5 tablespoons sliced almonds, divided
- ⅛ teaspoon ground cardamom
- ¼ cup blueberries

PREPARATION:

1. In a blender, combine banana, raspberries, almond milk, cinnamon, cardamom, 3 tablespoons almonds, and vanilla.

2. Transfer the smoothie into a bowl and top with blueberries, the remaining 2 tablespoons almonds and coconut.

NUTRITIONAL INFORMATION PER SERVING:

Calories		244
		% Daily Value*
Total Fat 9.3g		12%
Saturated Fat 1.5g		7%
Cholesterol 0mg		0%
Sodium 2mg		0%
Total Carbohydrate 37g		13%
Dietary Fiber 7.6g		27%
Total Sugars 25.5g		
Protein 6.9g		
Vitamin D 20mcg		100%
Calcium 133mg		10%
Iron 2mg		10%
Potassium 364mg		8%

YOGURT RASPBERRY CEREAL BOWL

Very Easy

5 minutes

1 Servings

INGREDIENTS:

- 1 cup nonfat plain yogurt
- ½ cup mini shredded-wheat cereal
- ¼ cup fresh raspberries
- 2 teaspoons mini chocolate chips
- 1 teaspoon pumpkin seeds
- ¼ teaspoon ground cinnamon

PREPARATION:

1. In a bowl, put some yogurt and top with raspberries, shredded wheat, chocolate chips, cinnamon, and pumpkin seeds.

NUTRITIONAL INFORMATION PER SERVING:

Calories		357
	% Daily Value*	
Total Fat 7.3g		9%
Saturated Fat 4g		20%
Cholesterol 15mg		5%
Sodium 215mg		9%
Total Carbohydrate 53.9g		20%
Dietary Fiber 6.9g		25%
Total Sugars 28.1g		
Protein 18.1g		
Vitamin D 0mcg		0%
Calcium 463mg		36%
Iron 9mg		52%
Potassium 753mg		16%

BREAKFAST SALAD WITH EGG & SALSA VERDE VINAIGRETTE

Easy

10 minutes

2 Servings

INGREDIENTS:

- 3 tablespoons salsa verde
- 2 tablespoons cilantro, chopped
- 8 blue corn tortilla chips, broken into large pieces
- ¼ avocado, sliced
- 1 tablespoon extra-virgin olive oil, divided
- 2 cups mesclun
- ½ cup canned red kidney beans, rinsed
- 1 large egg

PREPARATION:

1. In a bowl, combine salsa, half oil, and cilantro.
2. In another bowl, mingle mesclun with half the mixture.
3. Top with chips, followed by beans and avocado.
4. In a small skillet, fry egg in the remaining oil for about 2 minutes.
5. Serve the egg over the salad and trickle with remaining salsa vinaigrette to serve.

NUTRITIONAL INFORMATION PER SERVING:

Calories	380
	% Daily Value*
Total Fat 17g	22%
Saturated Fat 3.1g	16%
Cholesterol 93mg	31%
Sodium 255mg	11%
Total Carbohydrate 43g	16%
Dietary Fiber 12.2g	43%
Total Sugars 1.7g	
Protein 17.7g	
Vitamin D 9mcg	44%
Calcium 110mg	8%
Iron 5mg	26%
Potassium 795mg	17%

NUTRITIOUS EGG BAKE

Medium

30 minutes

2 Servings

INGREDIENTS:

- 4 large eggs, beaten
- 3½ ounces kale, thawed
- 4 tablespoons skimmed milk
- ¼ teaspoon dried thyme
- 2 pinches ground black pepper
- 1/8 cup sharp cheddar cheese, shredded
- ¼ teaspoon Dijon mustard
- ¼ teaspoon kosher salt
- 2 pinches ground nutmeg

PREPARATION:

1. Set the oven's temperature to 350 degrees F and coat a 9-inch pie tin with oil spray.
2. Place the kale in the prepared pie pan after squeezing the extra moisture from it.
3. In a mixing bowl, combine milk and eggs, salt, pepper, nutmeg, mustard, and thyme.
4. Drizzle the egg mixture on the kale, followed by cheddar cheese.
5. Bake for about 30 minutes and take out of the oven.
6. Serve after cutting each wedge into six pieces.

NUTRITIONAL INFORMATION PER SERVING:

Calories	211
	% Daily Value*
Total Fat 13.3g	17%
Saturated Fat 5.2g	26%
Cholesterol 383mg	128%
Sodium 621mg	27%
Total Carbohydrate 6.6g	2%
Dietary Fiber 0.8g	3%
Total Sugars 1.3g	
Protein 16.8g	
Vitamin D 36mcg	181%
Calcium 201mg	15%
Iron 3mg	16%
Potassium 385mg	8%

BLUEBERRY SMOOTHIE BOWL

Very Easy

10 minutes

2 Servings

INGREDIENTS:

- 2 cups fresh raspberries, divided
- 2 frozen bananas, peeled
- 1 tablespoon hemp seeds
- ½ cup almond milk, unsweetened

PREPARATION:

1. In a blender, add raspberries, bananas, hemp seeds, and almond milk and pulse well.
2. Shift the mixture into 2 serving bowls and serve with your favorite topping.

NUTRITIONAL INFORMATION PER SERVING:

	Calories	349
		% Daily Value*
	Total Fat 18.9g	24%
	Saturated Fat 13g	65%
	Cholesterol 0mg	0%
	Sodium 11mg	0%
	Total Carbohydrate 45.5g	17%
	Dietary Fiber 12.6g	45%
	Total Sugars 21.9g	
	Protein 6.6g	
	Vitamin D 0mcg	0%
	Calcium 51mg	4%
	Iron 3mg	17%
	Potassium 836mg	18%

BANANA AND PEANUT BUTTER PORRIDGE

Very Easy

10 minutes

2 Servings

INGREDIENTS:

- ½ tablespoon peanut butter, softened
- 2 large ripe bananas, peeled and mashed
- ¼ teaspoon ground cinnamon

PREPARATION:

1. In a large-sized bowl, add peanut butter, mashed bananas, and cinnamon.
2. Stir well and serve immediately.

NUTRITIONAL INFORMATION PER SERVING:

	Calories	146
		% Daily Value*
Total Fat 2.7g		3%
Saturated Fat 0.3g		2%
Cholesterol 0mg		0%
Sodium 2mg		0%
Total Carbohydrate 32g		12%
Dietary Fiber 4.1g		15%
Total Sugars 16.8g		
Protein 2.3g		
Vitamin D 0mcg		0%
Calcium 11mg		1%
Iron 1mg		6%
Potassium 518mg		11%

OVERNIGHT QUINOA PUDDING

Very Easy

5 minutes

2 Servings

INGREDIENTS:

- 1 cup quinoa, cooked and cooled
- ¾ cup plain kefir
- 1 tablespoon chia seeds
- 2 teaspoons pure maple syrup
- ¼ teaspoon vanilla extract
- Dash of ground cinnamon
- 1 cup fresh berries

PREPARATION:

1. In a bowl, combine quinoa with chia seeds, kefir, maple syrup, cinnamon, and vanilla.
2. Refrigerate overnight and serve topped with berries.

NUTRITIONAL INFORMATION PER SERVING:

Calories	431
	% Daily Value*
Total Fat 7.3g	9%
Saturated Fat 1.3g	6%
Cholesterol 4mg	1%
Sodium 53mg	2%
Total Carbohydrate 72.2g	26%
Dietary Fiber 10.5g	37%
Total Sugars 11.3g	
Protein 18.4g	
Vitamin D 38mcg	188%
Calcium 191mg	15%
Iron 5mg	26%
Potassium 598mg	13%

RASPBERRY OVERNIGHT MUESLI

Easy

15 minutes

1 Servings

INGREDIENTS:

- ¾ cup vanilla yogurt, nonfat
- ½ cup rolled oats, old-fashioned
- ½ cup fresh raspberries
- 1 tablespoon almonds, toasted chopped

PREPARATION:

1. In a medium bowl, combine yogurt and oats.
2. Refrigerate overnight and mix in the raspberries and almonds to serve.

NUTRITIONAL INFORMATION PER SERVING:

Calories	352
	% Daily Value*
Total Fat 8.3g	11%
Saturated Fat 2.5g	13%
Cholesterol 11mg	4%
Sodium 132mg	6%
Total Carbohydrate 49.3g	18%
Dietary Fiber 8.9g	32%
Total Sugars 16.3g	
Protein 17.8g	
Vitamin D 0mcg	0%
Calcium 389mg	30%
Iron 3mg	14%
Potassium 714mg	15%

Easy

15 minutes

2 Servings

INGREDIENTS:

- ½ cup part-skim ricotta cheese
- 2 whole-wheat bread slices
- 4 tablespoons fresh strawberries
- 2 teaspoons maple syrup
- 2 teaspoons almonds, sliced

PREPARATION:

1. Organize the slices of bread on serving platters.
2. Add strawberries, ricotta, and almonds on top of each slice.
3. Top with maple syrup to serve.

NUTRITIONAL INFORMATION PER SERVING:

Calories	195
	% Daily Value*
Total Fat 7.5g	10%
Saturated Fat 3.1g	16%
Cholesterol 19mg	6%
Sodium 228mg	10%
Total Carbohydrate 23.7g	9%
Dietary Fiber 2.7g	10%
Total Sugars 7g	
Protein 11.6g	
Vitamin D 0mcg	0%
Calcium 239mg	18%
Iron 1mg	8%
Potassium 120mg	3%

SPAGHETTI FRITTATA

Medium

10 minutes

2 Servings

INGREDIENTS:

- 2 eggs
- 1¼ cups milk, fat-free
- 1 teaspoon olive oil
- Black pepper, to taste
- 1 oz. mozzarella cheese, part-skim and shredded
- 1¼ cups spaghetti, whole-wheat, cooked
- 1 tablespoon fresh basil leaves, chopped
- 4 tablespoons scallion, chopped
- 1 egg white

PREPARATION:

1. In a bowl, combine eggs, egg white, and black pepper and beat until well combined.
2. In a non-stick skillet, put olive oil and cook the spaghetti for about 2 minutes over medium heat.
3. Top evenly with the egg mixture and sprinkle with cheese, scallion, and basil.
4. Cook for about 8 minutes and dish out in a platter to serve.

NUTRITIONAL INFORMATION PER SERVING:

Calories	246
	% Daily Value*
Total Fat 16g	20%
Saturated Fat 3.7g	19%
Cholesterol 327mg	109%
Sodium 202mg	9%
Total Carbohydrate 16.6g	6%
Dietary Fiber 2.9g	10%
Total Sugars 12.6g	
Protein 11.4g	
Vitamin D 31mcg	154%
Calcium 50mg	4%
Iron 2mg	12%
Potassium 241mg	5%

PUMPKIN OMELET

Easy

10 minutes

2 Servings

INGREDIENTS:

- 3 teaspoons olive oil, divided
- ¼ teaspoon ground cinnamon
- 1/8 teaspoon organic vanilla extract
- Pinch of salt
- 1 cup raw pumpkin, chopped
- 4 eggs

PREPARATION:

1. Put 1 teaspoon of olive oil along with pumpkin, cinnamon, and nutmeg in a nonstick frying pan over medium-low heat. Cook for about 5 minutes, rotating once.
2. Meanwhile, in a bowl, beat well eggs, vanilla extract, and salt until fluffy.
3. Add remaining olive oil in the pan and trickle this egg mixture over apple slices evenly.
4. Cook for about 4 minutes and fold the omelet to serve.

NUTRITIONAL INFORMATION PER SERVING:

Calories	262
	% Daily Value*
Total Fat 10.8g	14%
Saturated Fat 4.3g	21%
Cholesterol 165mg	55%
Sodium 198mg	9%
Total Carbohydrate 25.9g	9%
Dietary Fiber 3.4g	12%
Total Sugars 6.6g	
Protein 17.6g	
Vitamin D 15mcg	73%
Calcium 192mg	15%
Iron 2mg	9%
Potassium 198mg	4%

Oatmeal-Rhubarb Porridge

Easy

15 minutes

2 Servings

INGREDIENTS:

- ½ cup orange juice
- 1½ cups almond milk
- 1 cup rolled oats, old-fashioned
- ½ teaspoon ground cinnamon
- 3 tablespoons maple syrup
- 1 cup ½-inch pieces rhubarb, fresh or frozen
- Pinch of salt
- 2 tablespoons pecans, chopped

PREPARATION:

1. In a medium saucepan, combine almond milk, oats, juice, cinnamon, rhubarb, and salt.
2. Bring it to a thorough boil and then, switch the heat to low.
3. Cover with the lid and cook for about 5 minutes, frequently stirring.
4. Remove from heat and stir in the maple syrup.
5. Top with pecans and serve.

NUTRITIONAL INFORMATION PER SERVING:

Calories	787
	% Daily Value*
Total Fat 55.9g	72%
Saturated Fat 39.6g	198%
Cholesterol 0mg	0%
Sodium 113mg	5%
Total Carbohydrate 69.5g	25%
Dietary Fiber 11.1g	40%
Total Sugars 30.7g	
Protein 12g	
Vitamin D 0mcg	0%
Calcium 139mg	11%
Iron 6mg	35%
Potassium 1043mg	22%

AVOCADO AND BLACK BEAN EGGS

Easy

5 minutes

2 Servings

INGREDIENTS

- 1 red chilli, deseeded and thinly sliced
- 2 teaspoons rapeseed oil
- 1 large garlic clove, sliced
- 1 cup black beans
- ¼ teaspoon cumin seeds
- ½ cup fresh coriander, chopped
- 2 large eggs
- ½ can cherry tomatoes
- 1 small avocado, halved and sliced
- 1 lime, cut into wedges

PREPARATION

1. Put the rapeseed oil, chilli, and garlic in a non-stick frying pan and sauté for about 2 minutes.

2. Crack the eggs on both corners of the pan. Ladle the beans and tomatoes into the pan once they are firm, then top with the cumin seeds.

3. Eliminate the skillet from the heat and top with avocado and cilantro.

4. Squeeze the lime wedges over the top and serve.

NUTRITIONAL INFORMATION PER SERVING:

Calories	591	
		% Daily Value*
Total Fat 35.9g		46%
Saturated Fat 6.4g		32%
Cholesterol 186mg		62%
Sodium 829mg		36%
Total Carbohydrate 53.9g		20%
Dietary Fiber 18g		64%
Total Sugars 5.6g		
Protein 20.5g		
Vitamin D 18mcg		88%
Calcium 167mg		13%
Iron 7mg		38%
Potassium 1375mg		29%

MAPLE GLAZED TURKEY BREASTS

Easy

15 minutes

2 Servings

INGREDIENTS:

- 1/8 cup maple syrup
- 2 (4-oz.) boneless, skinless turkey breasts, pounded slightly
- 1/8 cup whole grain mustard
- ½ teaspoon garlic, minced
- 1 teaspoon olive oil

PREPARATION:

1. Set the oven's temperature to 425 °F and lightly grease a baking sheet.
2. In a bowl, combine well the maple syrup, mustard, oil and garlicups
3. Coat the turkey breasts evenly in this mixture and position them on the baking sheet.
4. Bake for about 15 minutes and eliminate from the oven to serve hot.

NUTRITIONAL INFORMATION PER SERVING:

Calories	298
	% Daily Value*
Total Fat 11.3g	14%
Saturated Fat 2.7g	13%
Cholesterol 101mg	34%
Sodium 167mg	7%
Total Carbohydrate 14.4g	5%
Dietary Fiber 0g	0%
Total Sugars 11.7g	
Protein 32.9g	
Vitamin D 0mcg	0%
Calcium 31mg	2%
Iron 2mg	9%
Potassium 319mg	7%

CHICKEN AND SPINACH CURRY

Easy

30 minutes

2 Servings

INGREDIENTS:

- 1 tablespoon salt-free curry paste
- ½ tablespoon olive oil
- ½ lb. skinless, boneless chicken breasts, cubed
- ½ cup chicken broth, salt-free
- Ground black pepper, to taste
- ½ cup coconut milk, unsweetened
- 1 cup spinach

PREPARATION:

1. In a non-stick wok, put olive oil and curry paste and sauté over medium heat for about 2 minutes.
2. Add the chicken and cook for about 10 minutes.
3. Add coconut milk and broth and heat until it is boiled.
4. Switch the heat low and cook for about 10 minutes.
5. Add spinach and black pepper and cook for about 5 minutes.
6. Dish out and serve hot.

NUTRITIONAL INFORMATION PER SERVING:

Calories	309	
	% Daily Value*	
Total Fat 21.3g		27%
Saturated Fat 14.4g		72%
Cholesterol 49mg		16%
Sodium 428mg		19%
Total Carbohydrate 9g		3%
Dietary Fiber 3.2g		11%
Total Sugars 3.4g		
Protein 22.6g		
Vitamin D 0mcg		0%
Calcium 42mg		3%
Iron 2mg		13%
Potassium 325mg		7%

OREGANO CHICKEN BREAST

Easy

16 minutes

2 Servings

INGREDIENTS:

- 2 (4-oz.) boneless, skinless chicken breasts, pounded slightly
- ½ tablespoon olive oil
- ½ teaspoon dried oregano
- ½ teaspoon paprika
- Pinch of salt
- Ground black pepper, to taste

PREPARATION:

1. Set the oven's temperature to 425 °F and lightly grease a baking dish.
2. In a bowl, merge together oregano, salt, and black pepper.
3. Scrub this mixture generously over chicken breasts.
4. Position the chicken breasts onto the prepared baking dish in a single layer.
5. Bake for about 15 minutes and remove from the oven to serve hot.

NUTRITIONAL INFORMATION PER SERVING:

Calories	248
	% Daily Value*
Total Fat 12g	15%
Saturated Fat 2.8g	14%
Cholesterol 101mg	34%
Sodium 137mg	6%
Total Carbohydrate 0.6g	0%
Dietary Fiber 0.4g	1%
Total Sugars 0.1g	
Protein 32.9g	
Vitamin D 0mcg	0%
Calcium 24mg	2%
Iron 2mg	9%
Potassium 295mg	6%

VEGAN SUPERFOOD GRAIN BOWLS

Easy

10 minutes

4 Servings

INGREDIENTS:

- ½ cup hummus
- 8 ounce quinoa, cooked
- 2 tablespoons lemon juice
- 2 cups whole baby beets, sliced and cooked
- 1 medium avocado, sliced
- 5 ounce baby kale
- 1 cup frozen shelled edamame, thawed
- ¼ cup sunflower seeds, unsalted and toasted

PREPARATION:

1. In a small bowl, merge hummus and lemon juice.
2. In small containers, divide the hummus-lemon mixture.
3. Put the kale in 4 serving plates and top wth quinoa, beets, edamame, and sunflower seeds.
4. Top with avocado and hummus dressing to serve.

NUTRITIONAL INFORMATION PER SERVING:

Calories	471
	% Daily Value*
Total Fat 20.4g	26%
Saturated Fat 3.4g	17%
Cholesterol 0mg	0%
Sodium 178mg	8%
Total Carbohydrate 57.2g	21%
Dietary Fiber 13.3g	48%
Total Sugars 3g	
Protein 20g	
Vitamin D 0mcg	0%
Calcium 144mg	11%
Iron 5mg	30%
Potassium 864mg	

CURRIED HALIBUT

Easy

25 minutes

2 Servings

INGREDIENTS:

- ½ onion, chopped
- ½ tablespoon olive oil
- 1 tablespoons curry powder
- 1½ garlic cloves, crushed
- 1 (400g) can chickpeas
- Zest of ½ lemon, cut into wedges
- 1 (½-inch) piece ginger, peeled and finely grated
- 1 cup tomatoes, chopped
- 2 halibut fillets
- ¼ cup coriander, roughly chopped

PREPARATION:

1. In a large frying pan, put the oil and onions, and sauté for about 3 minutes.
2. Stir in the curry powder, ginger, and garlic, and cook for another 2 minutes.
3. Add the tomatoes, chickpeas, and a pinch of salt and pepper.
4. Cook for about 10 minutes and add in the halibut.
5. Cook for another 5 minutes and top with coriander and lemon zest.
6. Serve and enjoy!

NUTRITIONAL INFORMATION PER SERVING:

Calories	306
	% Daily Value*
Total Fat 6.5g	8%
Saturated Fat 0.7g	3%
Cholesterol 55mg	18%
Sodium 437mg	19%
Total Carbohydrate 36.2g	13%
Dietary Fiber 8.2g	29%
Total Sugars 3.8g	
Protein 27.7g	
Vitamin D 0mcg	0%
Calcium 75mg	6%
Iron 3mg	17%
Potassium 534mg	11%

SPICED DUCK BREAST

Easy

12 minutes

2 Servings

INGREDIENTS:

- 1 tablespoon olive oil
- ½ teaspoon ground cumin
- ¼ teaspoon smoked paprika
- Pinch of salt
- Ground black pepper, as required
- 2 (4-oz.) duck breasts, boneless and skinless

PREPARATION:

1. Set the grill to medium-high heat and lightly grease the grill grate.
2. In a bowl, merge the olive oil, cumin, paprika, salt, and black pepper.
3. Scrub the duck breasts evenly with oil mixture.
4. Position the duck breasts onto the grill and grill for about 6 minutes per side.
5. Serve hot.

NUTRITIONAL INFORMATION PER SERVING:

Calories	278
	% Daily Value*
Total Fat 15.6g	20%
Saturated Fat 3.3g	17%
Cholesterol 101mg	34%
Sodium 176mg	8%
Total Carbohydrate 0.4g	0%
Dietary Fiber 0.2g	1%
Total Sugars 0g	
Protein 33g	
Vitamin D 0mcg	0%
Calcium 23mg	2%
Iron 2mg	10%
Potassium 292mg	6%

CHIMICHURRI NOODLE BOWLS

Medium

5 minutes

4 Servings

INGREDIENTS:

Chimichurri Sauce

- 2 cups fresh flat-leaf parsley
- 3 tablespoons lemon juice
- ½ teaspoon crushed red pepper
- ¼ teaspoon ground pepper
- 5 cloves garlic
- 1 teaspoon dried oregano
- ½ teaspoon salt
- ½ cup extra-virgin olive oil

Noodle Bowls

- 8 cups zucchini noodles
- 4 ounces whole-grain spaghetti, boiled
- 12 ounces shrimp, peeled and cooked
- ¼ cup crumbled feta cheese

PREPARATION:

1. For Chimichurri Sauce: In a food processor, bitz garlic, oil, parsley, lemon juice, crushed red pepper, oregano, salt, and pepper.
2. For Noodle Bowls: Organize spaghetti and zucchini noodles in a bowl and toss well.
3. Top with feta and shrimp.
4. Add in the chimichurri sauce and serve immediately.

NUTRITIONAL INFORMATION PER SERVING:

Calories	434
	% Daily Value*
Total Fat 29.6g	38%
Saturated Fat 5.7g	29%
Cholesterol 187mg	62%
Sodium 646mg	28%
Total Carbohydrate 20.6g	7%
Dietary Fiber 5.1g	18%
Total Sugars 5.1g	
Protein 26.2g	
Vitamin D 0mcg	0%
Calcium 218mg	17%
Iron 4mg	20%
Potassium 963mg	20%

CHICKEN WITH CASHEWS AND PINEAPPLES

Medium

25 minutes

2 Servings

INGREDIENTS:

- ¼ cup onions, chopped
- ¼ tablespoon olive oil, extra-virgin
- ¼ garlic clove, minced
- 1 oz. skinless, boneless chicken breasts, cubed
- ½ tomato, seeded and chopped
- ½ tablespoon soy sauce, low-sodium
- Ground black pepper, to taste
- ¼ teaspoon fresh ginger root, minced
- ½ cup cashew nuts
- ½ cup fresh pineapple, cubed
- 1 medium bell pepper, seeded and chopped
- ¼ tablespoon apple cider vinegar

PREPARATION:

1. In a non-stick wok, put olive oil and onions over medium heat and sauté for about 5 minutes.
2. Add garlic and ginger and sauté for about 1 minute.
3. Dump in the chicken and cook for about 5 minutes.
4. Add the pineapple, cashew nuts, tomatoes, and bell peppers and cook for about 6 minutes.
5. Drizzle in the soy sauce, vinegar and black pepper and cook for about 3 minutes.
6. Dish out and serve hot.

NUTRITIONAL INFORMATION PER SERVING:

Calories	183
	% Daily Value*
Total Fat 5.4g	7%
Saturated Fat 1.4g	7%
Cholesterol 44mg	15%
Sodium 333mg	14%
Total Carbohydrate 16.3g	6%
Dietary Fiber 2.7g	10%
Total Sugars 10.7g	
Protein 18.8g	
Vitamin D 0mcg	0%
Calcium 24mg	2%
Iron 1mg	7%
Potassium 322mg	7%

CHICKEN WITH HARISSA CHICKPEAS

Medium

10 minutes ·

2 Servings

INGREDIENTS:

- ½ onion, chopped
- 1 tablespoons rapeseed oil
- ½ red pepper, finely sliced
- 2 chicken breasts, bashed
- 1 can chickpeas
- ¾ tablespoon red harissa paste
- ½ yellow pepper, finely sliced
- ½ tablespoon za'atar
- ½ cup baby spinach, wilted
- ¼ small bunch of parsley, finely chopped

PREPARATION:

1. In a pan, put 1 tablespoon of rapeseed oil and pan-fry the onions and peppers for 7 minutes over medium heat.
2. Scrub the remaining oil and the za'atar mixture over chicken breasts and dust with salt and pepper.
3. Increase the grill's temperature and grill the chicken for 4 minutes on each side.
4. In a skillet, merge the chickpeas with the harissa paste and 2 tablespoons water.
5. Cook until warmed and mash well.
6. Toss the chickpeas with the pepper and onion mixture, spinach, and parsley.
7. Serve with sliced chicken on the side.

NUTRITIONAL INFORMATION PER SERVING:

Calories	753
	% Daily Value*
Total Fat 24.6g	32%
Saturated Fat 4.2g	21%
Cholesterol 130mg	43%
Sodium 170mg	7%
Total Carbohydrate 69.6g	25%
Dietary Fiber 19.5g	70%
Total Sugars 13.5g	
Protein 63.5g	
Vitamin D 0mcg	0%
Calcium 159mg	12%
Iron 9mg	51%
Potassium 1508mg	32%

MIXED GREENS WITH LENTILS & SLICED APPLE

Easy

20 minutes

2 Servings

INGREDIENTS:

- 1½ cups mixed salad greens
- ½ cup cooked lentils
- 1 apple, cored and sliced, divided
- 1½ tablespoons crumbled feta cheese
- 1 tablespoon red-wine vinegar
- 2 teaspoons extra-virgin olive oil

PREPARATION:

1. Organize mixed salad greens and top with lentils, feta and half apple slices.
2. Trickle with oil and vinegar.
3. Garnish remaining apple slices over top and serve.

NUTRITIONAL INFORMATION PER SERVING:

Calories	304
	% Daily Value*
Total Fat 7g	9%
Saturated Fat 1.8g	9%
Cholesterol 6mg	2%
Sodium 109mg	5%
Total Carbohydrate 47.9g	17%
Dietary Fiber 17.3g	62%
Total Sugars 12.9g	
Protein 15g	
Vitamin D 0mcg	0%
Calcium 76mg	6%
Iron 5mg	27%
Potassium 761mg	16%

CHIPOTLE-LIME CAULIFLOWER TACO BOWLS

Easy

10 minutes

4 Servings

INGREDIENTS:

- ¼ cup lime juice
- 2 tablespoons chipotles in adobo sauce, chopped
- 1 tablespoon honey
- 1 red onion, thinly sliced
- 1 cup red cabbage, shredded
- 2 garlic cloves
- 2 cups cooked quinoa, cooled
- 1 medium avocado
- ½ teaspoon salt
- 1 cup no-salt-added canned black beans, rinsed
- 1 lime, cut into 4 wedges
- 1 head cauliflower, cut into bite-size pieces
- ½ cup queso fresco, crumbled

PREPARATION:

1. Set the oven's temperature to 450 degrees F and lightly grease a baking sheet.
2. In a bowl, merge chipotles, honey, lime juice, garlic and salt.
3. In a large bowl, coat the cauliflower with sauce and move to the baking sheet.
4. Top with onion and roast for about 20 minutes.
5. Organize quinoa into 4 serving bowls and top with the cauliflower mixture, black beans, and cheese to serve.

NUTRITIONAL INFORMATION PER SERVING:

Calories	509
	% Daily Value*
Total Fat 11.6g	15%
Saturated Fat 2.5g	13%
Cholesterol 0mg	0%
Sodium 151mg	7%
Total Carbohydrate 76.9g	28%
Dietary Fiber 20.7g	74%
Total Sugars 4g	
Protein 28.2g	
Vitamin D 0mcg	0%
Calcium 279mg	21%
Iron 12mg	64%
Potassium 2132mg	45%

DINNER RECIPES

BEEF STUFFED TOMATOES

Medium

15 minutes

2 Servings

INGREDIENTS

- 6 oz. beef, cooked and shredded
- ½ cup celery, minced
- 3 teaspoons mayonnaise, low-fat
- 1 teaspoon olive oil, extra-virgin
- ¼ cup chickpeas, cooked
- ½ cup onion, minced
- 3 teaspoons plain Greek yogurt, fat-free
- 1 teaspoon mustard
- Black pepper, to taste
- 2 large tomatoes, halved and seeded

PREPARATION

1. In a bowl, merge all the ingredients thoroughly except tomatoes.
2. Stuff the beef mixture evenly in the tomato halves.
3. Serve immediately.

NUTRITIONAL INFORMATION PER SERVING:

Calories	384
	% Daily Value*
Total Fat 12.5g	16%
Saturated Fat 2.9g	15%
Cholesterol 78mg	26%
Sodium 145mg	6%
Total Carbohydrate 30.6g	11%
Dietary Fiber 7.8g	28%
Total Sugars 11.1g	
Protein 38.2g	
Vitamin D 0mcg	0%
Calcium 77mg	6%
Iron 18mg	102%
Potassium 1113mg	24%

CHICKEN AND GREEN BEAN CASSEROLE

Easy

45 minutes

2 Servings

INGREDIENTS:

- 1 lb. green beans, trimmed
- 1½ tablespoons olive oil, extra-virgin
- 1½ garlic cloves, minced
- 1½ chicken thighs, skinless and boneless
- ¼ teaspoon dried rosemary, crushed
- ¼ teaspoon dried oregano, crushed
- Black pepper, to taste

PREPARATION:

1. Set the temperature of the oven to 375 °F and lightly grease a large baking dish.
2. Take a large bowl and toss in all the ingredients to coat well.
3. Now, position the green beans at the bottom of the dish and layer it with chicken breasts.
4. Bake for about 45 minutes and remove from the oven to serve.

NUTRITIONAL INFORMATION PER SERVING:

Calories	310
	% Daily Value*
Total Fat 18.5g	24%
Saturated Fat 3.7g	18%
Cholesterol 93mg	31%
Sodium 106mg	5%
Total Carbohydrate 4g	1%
Dietary Fiber 1.4g	5%
Total Sugars 0.8g	
Protein 31.8g	
Vitamin D 0mcg	0%
Calcium 46mg	4%
Iron 2mg	10%
Potassium 413mg	9%

TURKEY AND STRAWBERRY LETTUCE WRAPS

Easy

30 minutes

2 Servings

INGREDIENTS:

- 6 oz. cooked turkey, cut into strips
- ½ cup fresh strawberries, hulled and thinly sliced
- 1 small cucumber, thinly sliced
- 1 tablespoon fresh mint leaves, minced
- 4 large lettuce leaves

PREPARATION:

1. In a glass bowl, merge all the ingredients except for lettuce leaves and gently toss to coat well.
2. Position the lettuce leaves onto serving plates.
3. Divide the turkey mixture evenly over each leaf and serve immediately.

NUTRITIONAL INFORMATION PER SERVING:

Calories	201
	% Daily Value*
Total Fat 6.7g	9%
Saturated Fat 1.8g	9%
Cholesterol 76mg	25%
Sodium 79mg	3%
Total Carbohydrate 9.4g	3%
Dietary Fiber 1.9g	7%
Total Sugars 4.6g	
Protein 26.1g	
Vitamin D 0mcg	0%
Calcium 49mg	4%
Iron 3mg	15%
Potassium 538mg	11%

GARLIC PRIME RIB ROAST

Easy

1 hour 35 minutes

2 Servings

INGREDIENTS:

- ¼ teaspoon dried thyme, crushed
- 1 garlic clove, minced
- 1/8 prime rib roast
- Pinch of salt
- Black pepper, to taste

PREPARATION:

1. Set the oven's temperature to 500 °F and lightly grease a roasting pan.
2. In a bowl, merge garlic, thyme, oil, salt, and black pepper.
3. Scrub the garlic mixture evenly on the rib roast.
4. Position the roast in a large roasting pan, fatty side up and marinate for one hour.
5. Move into the oven and roast for about 20 minutes.
6. Now, switch the temperature to 325° F and roast for about 75 minutes.
7. Eliminate from the oven and place the rib roast onto a cutting board.
8. Carve the rib coast into desired sized slices and serve.

NUTRITIONAL INFORMATION PER SERVING:

Calories	242	
	% Daily Value*	
Total Fat 17.9g	23%	
Saturated Fat 7.1g	36%	
Cholesterol 60mg	20%	
Sodium 583mg	25%	
Total Carbohydrate 2g	1%	
Dietary Fiber 0.1g	0%	
Total Sugars 0g		
Protein 16.8g		
Vitamin D 0mcg	0%	
Calcium 7mg	1%	
Iron 0mg	1%	
Potassium 10mg	0%	

LEMONY PORK TENDERLOIN

Easy

30 minutes

2 Servings

INGREDIENTS:

- ¼ cup fresh mixed herbs, chopped
- 1 garlic clove, minced
- ¼ teaspoon fresh lemon zest, grated
- ¼ tablespoon fresh lemon juice
- Black pepper, to taste
- 1½ tablespoons olive oil
- Pinch of salt
- ½ lb. pork tenderloin

PREPARATION:

1. Set the oven's temperature to 425 degrees °F and lightly grease a baking sheet.
2. In a large-sized bowl, merge all the ingredients thoroughly except the pork tenderloin.
3. Add the pork tenderloin and coat generously with the herb mixture.
4. Refrigerate to marinate for about 45 minutes.
5. Position the pork tenderloin on the baking sheet and bake for about 30 minutes.
6. Eliminate from the oven and carve into desired slices before serving.

NUTRITIONAL INFORMATION PER SERVING:

Calories	387
	% Daily Value*
Total Fat 22g	28%
Saturated Fat 6.4g	32%
Cholesterol 136mg	45%
Sodium 104mg	5%
Total Carbohydrate 2.6g	1%
Dietary Fiber 1.4g	5%
Total Sugars 0.2g	
Protein 43.3g	
Vitamin D 0mcg	0%
Calcium 97mg	7%
Iron 4mg	24%
Potassium 652mg	14%

RAINBOW GRAIN BOWL WITH CASHEW TAHINI SAUCE

Easy

20 minutes

2 Servings

INGREDIENTS:

- ½ cup water
- ¾ cup cashews, unsalted
- ¼ cup parsley leaves, packed
- 1 tablespoon olive oil, extra-virgin
- ¼ teaspoon salt
- ½ cup quinoa, cooked
- ¼ cup raw beet, grated
- ¼ cup carrot, grated
- 1 tablespoon cashews, toasted chopped
- 1 tablespoon cider vinegar
- ½ teaspoon reduced-sodium tamari
- ½ cup lentils, cooked
- ½ cup red cabbage, shredded
- ¼ cup bell pepper, chopped
- ¼ cup cucumber, sliced

PREPARATION:

1. In a blender, blitz cashews, water, parsley, lemon juice, oil, tamari, and salt.
2. In a serving bowl, organize quinoa and lentils.
3. Top with beet, cabbage, pepper, cucumber, and carrot.
4. Put 2 tablespoons of the cashew sauce over the top.
5. Serve garnished with cashews.

NUTRITIONAL INFORMATION PER SERVING:

Calories	810
	% Daily Value*
Total Fat 42g	54%
Saturated Fat 7.7g	38%
Cholesterol 0mg	0%
Sodium 427mg	19%
Total Carbohydrate 85.2g	31%
Dietary Fiber 21.4g	77%
Total Sugars 8.4g	
Protein 30.2g	
Vitamin D 0mcg	0%
Calcium 109mg	8%
Iron 11mg	59%
Potassium 1321mg	28%

BEEF BRISKET

Medium

15 minutes

8 Servings

INGREDIENTS:

- 1 tablespoon olive oil
- 2½ pounds beef brisket, sliced
- Black pepper, to taste
- 1½ cups chopped onions
- 4 garlic cloves, smashed and peeled
- 1 teaspoon dried thyme
- 1 can (14.5 ounces) no-salt-added tomatoes and liquid
- ¼ cup red wine vinegar
- 1 cup red wine

PREPARATION:

1. Set the oven's temperature to 350 °F and lightly grease a baking sheet.
2. Dust beef brisket with pepper and sear in 1 tablespoon oil over medium-high heat.
3. Cook meat for about 6 minutes, occasionally turning.
4. Dish out the brisket in a plate.
5. Add onions, garlic and thyme to the pot and cook for about 4 minutes.
6. Add tomatoes, vinegar, and wine and thoroughly boil.
7. Add beef to the pot and fasten the lid.
8. Move the pot in the oven and cook for about 3 hours.
9. Dish out and serve warm.

NUTRITIONAL INFORMATION PER SERVING:

Calories	325
	% Daily Value*
Total Fat 10.7g	14%
Saturated Fat 3.6g	18%
Cholesterol 127mg	42%
Sodium 99mg	4%
Total Carbohydrate 5.5g	2%
Dietary Fiber 1.2g	4%
Total Sugars 2.5g	
Protein 43.8g	
Vitamin D 0mcg	0%
Calcium 20mg	2%
Iron 27mg	151%
Potassium 766mg	16%

LEMONY COD

Easy

10 minutes

2 Servings

INGREDIENTS:

- ½ tablespoon fresh lemon zest, grated
- 1 garlic clove, minced
- 1 tablespoon olive oil, extra-virgin
- ½ pinch of salt
- 2 (4-oz.) cod fillets, boneless and skinless
- 1 tablespoon fresh lemon juice
- Black pepper, to taste

PREPARATION:

1. Set the grill to medium-high heat and lightly grease the grill grate.
2. In a bowl, merge all the ingredients and toss well.
3. Position the cod fillets onto the grill and cook for about 5 minutes per side.
4. Dish out and serve hot.

NUTRITIONAL INFORMATION PER SERVING:

Calories	215	
	% Daily Value*	
Total Fat 14.1g	18%	
Saturated Fat 2.1g	10%	
Cholesterol 50mg	17%	
Sodium 91mg	4%	
Total Carbohydrate 1g	0%	
Dietary Fiber 0.2g	1%	
Total Sugars 0.3g		
Protein 22.2g		
Vitamin D 0mcg	0%	
Calcium 44mg	3%	
Iron 1mg	4%	
Potassium 456mg	10%	

HERBED FLANK STEAK

Easy

10 minutes

2 Servings

INGREDIENTS:

- 2 (4-oz.) flank steaks, trimmed
- 1 tablespoon olive oil, extra-virgin
- 1 teaspoon fresh basil
- 1½ tablespoons fresh rosemary, chopped
- Black pepper, as required
- 1 pinch of salt

PREPARATION:

1. Dust the steaks with rosemary, basil, salt and black pepper.
2. In a non-stick wok, put the olive oil and seasoned steaks and cook the steaks with for about 5 minutes per side over medium-high heat.
3. Dish out in a platter and serve immediately.

NUTRITIONAL INFORMATION PER SERVING:

Calories	288
	% Daily Value*
Total Fat 16.8g	22%
Saturated Fat 5.1g	25%
Cholesterol 62mg	21%
Sodium 104mg	5%
Total Carbohydrate 1.6g	1%
Dietary Fiber 1.1g	4%
Total Sugars 0g	
Protein 31.7g	
Vitamin D 0mcg	0%
Calcium 49mg	4%
Iron 3mg	16%
Potassium 407mg	9%

LAMB WITH BRUSSELS SPROUT

Easy

15 minutes

2 Servings

INGREDIENTS:

- ½ lb. lamb meat, trimmed and chopped
- ½ tablespoon olive oil
- ¼ lb. Brussels sprouts, trimmed and halved
- 1 tablespoon low-sodium soy sauce
- Ground black pepper, as required
- ½ garlic cloves, minced
- ¼ tablespoon balsamic vinegar
- ¼ scallion, sliced

PREPARATION:

1. In a non-stick wok, put olive oil and lamb and cook for about 4 minutes over medium-high heat.
2. Add Brussels sprouts and garlic and stir fry for about 4 minutes.
3. Sprinkle in the soy sauce, vinegar, and black pepper and cook for about 2 minutes.
4. Stir in the scallion and dish out to serve hot.

NUTRITIONAL INFORMATION PER SERVING:

Calories	212
	% Daily Value*
Total Fat 8.3g	11%
Saturated Fat 1.9g	9%
Cholesterol 69mg	23%
Sodium 367mg	16%
Total Carbohydrate 7.7g	3%
Dietary Fiber 2.9g	11%
Total Sugars 2g	
Protein 27.8g	
Vitamin D 0mcg	0%
Calcium 35mg	3%
Iron 2mg	12%
Potassium 705mg	15%

ROSEMARY PORK TENDERLOIN

Easy

50 minutes

2 Servings

INGREDIENTS:

- 1 garlic clove, minced
- ¼-lb. pork tenderloin, trimmed
- ¼ tablespoon fresh rosemary, minced
- Ground black pepper, as required
- Pinch of salt
- ¼ tablespoon olive oil

PREPARATION:

1. Set the oven's temperature to 500 °F and lightly grease a roasting pan.
2. Position the pork tenderloin into the roasting pan.
3. Scrub the roast with garlic, rosemary, salt, and black pepper, and trickle with oil.
4. Move into the oven and roast for about 50 minutes.
5. Eliminate from the oven and carve into desired slices before serving.

NUTRITIONAL INFORMATION PER SERVING:

Calories	246
	% Daily Value*
Total Fat 11.6g	15%
Saturated Fat 4.1g	21%
Cholesterol 104mg	35%
Sodium 79mg	3%
Total Carbohydrate 0.5g	0%
Dietary Fiber 0.1g	1%
Total Sugars 0g	
Protein 32.9g	
Vitamin D 0mcg	0%
Calcium 24mg	2%
Iron 2mg	13%
Potassium 412mg	9%

GARLICKY HADDOCK

 Easy

 10 minutes

 2 Servings

INGREDIENTS:

- 1 tablespoon olive oil
- 2 (4-oz.) haddock fillets, skinless
- 1½ garlic cloves, minced
- 1½ tablespoons chicken broth, salt-free
- Pinch of salt
- Ground black pepper, to taste

PREPARATION:

1. Put olive oil and haddock fillets in a large wok and cook for about 3 minutes over medium heat.
2. Flip the side and stir in the garlicups
3. Cook for about 2 minutes and stir in the broth.
4. Add the broth and cook for about 3 minutes.
5. Dish out and serve hot.

NUTRITIONAL INFORMATION PER SERVING:

Calories	159
	% Daily Value*
Total Fat 8.1g	10%
Saturated Fat 1.5g	7%
Cholesterol 55mg	18%
Sodium 115mg	5%
Total Carbohydrate 0.8g	0%
Dietary Fiber 0.1g	0%
Total Sugars 0.1g	
Protein 21.5g	
Vitamin D 0mcg	0%
Calcium 25mg	2%
Iron 1mg	7%
Potassium 19mg	0%

SMOOTHIES

CHOCOLATE-BANANA PROTEIN SMOOTHIE

Very Easy

5 minutes

2 Servings

INGREDIENTS:

- ½ cup cooked red lentils
- 1 banana, frozen
- ½ cup nonfat milk
- 1 teaspoon pure maple syrup
- 2 teaspoons cocoa powder, unsweetened

PREPARATION:

1. Merge all the ingredients and add to the blender.
2. Blend well and serve!

Variation Tip:

You can add the ice.

NUTRITIONAL INFORMATION PER SERVING:

Calories	515
	% Daily Value*
Total Fat 1.9g	2%
Saturated Fat 0.6g	3%
Cholesterol 2mg	1%
Sodium 73mg	3%
Total Carbohydrate 97.1g	35%
Dietary Fiber 33.6g	120%
Total Sugars 26.4g	
Protein 30.8g	

CANTALOUPE-WATERMELON SMOOTHIE

Very Easy

5 minutes

2 Servings

INGREDIENTS:

- 1 cup cantaloupe, cut-up
- 1½ cups watermelon seeded, cut-up
- ½ cup plain yogurt, low-fat
- 1 wedge cantaloupe
- ¼ cup orange juice

PREPARATION:

1. Merge all the ingredients and add to the blender.
2. Blend well and serve!

Variation Tip:

You can use any fruit juice.

NUTRITIONAL INFORMATION PER SERVING:

Calories	114
	% Daily Value*
Total Fat 1g	1%
Saturated Fat 0.7g	3%
Cholesterol 4mg	1%
Sodium 59mg	3%
Total Carbohydrate 24g	9%
Dietary Fiber 1.5g	5%
Total Sugars 22.4g	
Protein 4.7g	
Vitamin D 0mcg	0%
Calcium 127mg	10%
Iron 1mg	5%
Potassium 500mg	11%

MANGO-GINGER SMOOTHIE

Very Easy

5 minutes

1 Servings

INGREDIENTS:

- 1 cup mango chunks, frozen
- ½ cup cooked red lentils, cooled
- ¾ cup carrot juice
- 1 teaspoon honey
- 3 ice cubes
- 1 teaspoon fresh ginger, chopped
- Pinch of ground cardamom

PREPARATION:

1. Merge mango, lentils, carrot juice, honey, ginger, cardamom and ice cubes and add to the blender.
2. Blend well and serve!

Variation Tip:

You can gatnish with more cardamom for enhanced deliciousness.

NUTRITIONAL INFORMATION PER SERVING:

Calories	500
	% Daily Value*
Total Fat 1.8g	2%
Saturated Fat 0.3g	2%
Cholesterol 0mg	0%
Sodium 65mg	3%
Total Carbohydrate 97.7g	36%
Dietary Fiber 34.3g	122%
Total Sugars 34.4g	
Protein 27g	

BEET-WATERMELON-BANANA SMOOTHIE

Very Easy

5 minutes

2 Servings

INGREDIENTS:

- ½ medium-sized beet, chopped
- 1 watermelon slice, seeds removed and diced
- ½ banana, sliced
- 3 raw nuts
- ½ teaspoon ginger
- 1 orange slice
- ½ teaspoon cinnamon
- ½ lemon

PREPARATION:

1. Freeze the watermelon beets, and banana slices overnight.
2. Transfer the watermelon , beets, and banana slices into the blender along with the remaining ingredients.
3. Blend until smooth and ladle into glasses to serve.

Variation Tip:

You can also add some skimmed milk.

NUTRITIONAL INFORMATION PER SERVING:

Calories	137
	% Daily Value*
Total Fat 4.1g	5%
Saturated Fat 0.6g	3%
Cholesterol 0mg	0%
Sodium 69mg	3%
Total Carbohydrate 25.5g	9%
Dietary Fiber 3.5g	12%
Total Sugars 17g	
Protein 3.1g	
Vitamin D 0mcg	0%
Calcium 37mg	3%
Iron 1mg	6%
Potassium 438mg	9%

FRUIT AND YOGURT SMOOTHIE

Very Easy

10 minutes

2 Servings

INGREDIENTS:

- ¾ cup plain yogurt, non-fat
- ½ cup fruit juice, 100% pure
- ½ cup frozen blueberries
- ½ cup frozen raspberries
- ½ cup frozen pineapple
- ½ cup frozen peaches

PREPARATION:

1. Merge all the ingredients and add to the blender.
2. Blend well and serve!

Variation Tip:

You can use both the fresh or frozen banana.

NUTRITIONAL INFORMATION PER SERVING:

Calories	246
	% Daily Value*
Total Fat 1.6g	2%
Saturated Fat 1g	5%
Cholesterol 6mg	2%
Sodium 69mg	3%
Total Carbohydrate 52.2g	19%
Dietary Fiber 5g	18%
Total Sugars 46.1g	
Protein 6.6g	

BERRIE-BERRIE SMOOTHIE

Very Easy

5 minutes

2 Servings

INGREDIENTS:

- ½ cup skimmed milk
- 1 bowl raspberries, frozen
- ½ cup water
- 1 tablespoon lemon juice
- 5 medium strawberries, chopped

PREPARATION:

1. Merge all the ingredients and add to the blender.
2. Blend well and serve!

Variation Tip:

You can also add 1 teaspoon of coconut.

NUTRITIONAL INFORMATION PER SERVING:

Calories	167
	% Daily Value*
Total Fat 1.4g	2%
Saturated Fat 0.8g	4%
Cholesterol 5mg	2%
Sodium 32mg	1%
Total Carbohydrate 25g	9%
Dietary Fiber 0.6g	2%
Total Sugars 4.4g	
Protein 2.3g	
Vitamin D 0mcg	2%
Calcium 80mg	6%
Iron 0mg	1%
Potassium 91mg	2%

SALADS

CHICKEN AND VEGGIE TORTELLINI SALAD

Very Easy

10 minutes

2 Servings

INGREDIENTS:

- ¼ pound cooked chicken breast, sliced
- ½ bay leaves
- ¼ package cheese tortellini, boiled
- 1/8 cup green peas
- 1/8 cup ranch sauce
- ¼ tablespoon red-wine vinegar
- 2 tablespoons basil, chopped
- 1/8 cup artichokes, divided and chopped
- 1/8 cup radishes, julienned
- ¼ cup peas, boiled
- ½ tablespoon sunflower seeds

PREPARATION:

1. In a large-sized salad bowl, merge all the ingredients and gently toss to coat.
2. Serve immediately.

Variation Tip:

You can also use apple cider vinegar instead of red-wine vinegar.

NUTRITIONAL INFORMATION PER SERVING:

Calories	168
	% Daily Value*
Total Fat 4.2g	5%
Saturated Fat 0.2g	1%
Cholesterol 52mg	17%
Sodium 114mg	5%
Total Carbohydrate 12.3g	4%
Dietary Fiber 1.5g	5%
Total Sugars 1.1g	
Protein 19.4g	
Vitamin D 0mcg	0%
Calcium 20mg	2%
Iron 1mg	5%
Potassium 385mg	8%

LIME EGG VEGETABLE SALAD

Very Easy

30 minutes

2 Servings

INGREDIENTS:

- 3 tablespoons olive oil, extra-virgin
- 3 tablespoons canola oil
- 1 tablespoon lime juice
- 1/8 teaspoon salt
- ½ cup mixed vegetables, steamed
- ¼ small bunch watercress, large stems removed
- ¼ onion, rings
- ½ tablespoon cilantro, chopped
- ¼ teaspoon ground pepper
- 2 leaves lettuce
- ½ hard-boiled large egg, sliced

PREPARATION:

1. In a large-sized salad bowl, merge all the ingredients and gently toss to coat.
2. Serve immediately.

Variation Tip:

You can use rapeseed oil instead.

NUTRITIONAL INFORMATION PER SERVING:

Calories	207
	% Daily Value*
Total Fat 18.4g	24%
Saturated Fat 2.1g	10%
Cholesterol 29mg	10%
Sodium 392mg	17%
Total Carbohydrate 9.8g	4%
Dietary Fiber 3.7g	13%
Total Sugars 1.4g	
Protein 2.7g	
Vitamin D 0mcg	1%
Calcium 36mg	3%
Iron 1mg	5%
Potassium 194mg	4%

MANGO AND AVOCADO SALAD

Easy

15 minutes

2 Servings

INGREDIENTS:

- 1¼ cups avocado, peeled, pitted and sliced
- 1¼ cups mango, peeled, pitted and sliced
- ½ red onion, sliced
- ¼ cup fresh mint leaves, chopped
- Pinch of salt
- 3 cups fresh baby arugula
- 1 tablespoon fresh orange juice

PREPARATION:

1. Merge all the ingredients in a large serving bowl and toss gently.
2. Cover and refrigerate to chill before serving.

Variation Tip:

You can use rapeseed oil instead.

NUTRITIONAL INFORMATION PER SERVING:

Calories	275
	% Daily Value*
Total Fat 18.5g	24%
Saturated Fat 3.9g	19%
Cholesterol 0mg	0%
Sodium 97mg	4%
Total Carbohydrate 28.7g	10%
Dietary Fiber 9.6g	34%
Total Sugars 17g	
Protein 4.1g	
Vitamin D 0mcg	0%
Calcium 99mg	8%
Iron 3mg	15%
Potassium 834mg	18%

ORANGE AND BEET SALAD

Very Easy

15 minutes

2 Servings

INGREDIENTS:

- 1 large orange, peeled, seeded and sectioned
- 1½ beets, trimmed, peeled and sliced
- 2 cups fresh baby arugula
- 1/8 cup pecans, chopped
- 1½ tablespoons olive oil
- 1 pinch of salt

PREPARATION:

1. In a large-sized salad bowl, merge all the ingredients and gently toss to coat.
2. Serve immediately.

Variation Tip:

You can use rapeseed oil instead.

NUTRITIONAL INFORMATION PER SERVING:

Calories	194
	% Daily Value*
Total Fat 13g	17%
Saturated Fat 1.8g	9%
Cholesterol 0mg	0%
Sodium 102mg	4%
Total Carbohydrate 19.4g	7%
Dietary Fiber 4.3g	15%
Total Sugars 15g	
Protein 3.1g	
Vitamin D 0mcg	0%
Calcium 83mg	6%
Iron 1mg	6%
Potassium 469mg	10%

POWER SALAD WITH CHICKPEAS AND TUNA

Easy

10 minutes

4 Servings

INGREDIENTS:

- 3 cups kale, chopped
- 2 tablespoons honey-mustard vinaigrette
- 1 (2½-ounce) pouch tuna in water
- ½ cup chickpeas, rinsed and canned
- 1 carrot, peeled and shredded

PREPARATION:

1. In a bowl, merge kale with dressing and then, move into the mason jar.
2. Top with chickpeas, tuna, and carrot.
3. Fasten the mason jar lid and refrigerate for a minimum of 2 days.
4. In a bowl, dish out the jar contents and mix well before serving.

Variation Tip:

You can also use apple cider vinegar instead of honey-mustard vinaigrette.

NUTRITIONAL INFORMATION PER SERVING:

Calories	159
	% Daily Value*
Total Fat 3.3g	4%
Saturated Fat 0.4g	2%
Cholesterol 9mg	3%
Sodium 188mg	8%
Total Carbohydrate 23.4g	9%
Dietary Fiber 5.5g	20%
Total Sugars 4.4g	
Protein 10.5g	
Vitamin D 0mcg	0%
Calcium 99mg	8%
Iron 3mg	14%
Potassium 559mg	12%

GOAT CHEESE AND FIG SALAD

Very Easy

15 minutes

4 Servings

INGREDIENTS:

- 4 cups mixed salad greens
- 2 ounces fresh goat cheese, crumbled
- 8 dried figs, stemmed and sliced
- 3 tablespoons slivered almonds, preferably toasted
- 4 teaspoons olive oil, extra-virgin
- 1 teaspoon honey
- Black pepper, to taste
- 4 teaspoons balsamic vinegar
- Pinch of salt

PREPARATION:

1. In a mixing dish, merge the greens, figs, goat cheese, and almonds.
2. Mingle the olive oil, vinegar, honey, salt, and black pepper in another bowl.
3. Drizzle this dressing over the salad and serve.

Variation Tip:

You can add vegetables of your choice.

NUTRITIONAL INFORMATION PER SERVING:

Calories	506
	% Daily Value*
Total Fat 24.8g	32%
Saturated Fat 8.8g	44%
Cholesterol 30mg	10%
Sodium 334mg	15%
Total Carbohydrate 63g	23%
Dietary Fiber 8.6g	31%
Total Sugars 40.3g	
Protein 16.5g	
Vitamin D 0mcg	0%
Calcium 438mg	34%
Iron 4mg	23%
Potassium 1083mg	23%

Stuffed Poblano Peppers

Easy

30 minutes

2 Servings

INGREDIENTS:

- 2 large poblano peppers
- ¾ cup Fresh Grilled salsa
- ½ (15-ounce) can cooked black beans
- ¾ cup frozen corn
- ¼ cup uncooked brown rice
- ½ teaspoon cumin
- ½ teaspoon red chilli powder
- Black pepper, to taste
- ¼ cup 2% Mexican blend cheese, shredded
- 2 pinches cayenne pepper

PREPARATION:

1. Cook brown rice as directed on the packet.
2. Wash poblano pepper and remove the seeds and ribs. Slice it in half lengthwise.
3. Place the pepper in a baking dish. Broil for 3-5 minutes, then rotate the peppers and broil for another 3-5 minutes.
4. Drain and rinse black beans. Combine them with salsa, corn, quarter cups of cheese, cumin, chilli powder, and cayenne in a bowl.
5. Season with salt and pepper to taste. Microwave the filling for about 2-3 minutes, or until warm, stirring after each 30-second increment. Add the rice and mix well.
6. Fill each pepper half with the filling. Add remaining cheese and broil until the cheese has melted.
7. Serve and enjoy!

NUTRITIONAL INFORMATION PER SERVING:

Calories	265
	% Daily Value*
Total Fat 6.7g	9%
Saturated Fat 3.5g	17%
Cholesterol 18mg	6%
Sodium 552mg	24%
Total Carbohydrate 40.4g	15%
Dietary Fiber 3.2g	12%
Total Sugars 5g	
Protein 8.4g	
Vitamin D 0mcg	0%
Calcium 198mg	15%
Iron 3mg	17%
Potassium 401mg	9%

Easy

30 minutes

2 Servings

INGREDIENTS:

- ½ large eggplant
- ¼ teaspoon ground cumin
- ¼ teaspoon ground coriander
- Pinch of ground nutmeg
- Pinch of ground ginger
- ½ tablespoon olive oil
- ½ teaspoon mustard seed
- ¼ teaspoon curry powder
- 2 pinches salt
- 2 pinches black pepper
- ¼ yellow onion, finely chopped
- ½ garlic clove, minced
- 1 cup cherry tomatoes
- ½ tablespoon light molasses
- ½ teaspoon red wine vinegar
- ½ tablespoon chopped fresh cilantro

PREPARATION:

1. Slice the eggs about ¼-inch thick. Heat the grill pan and arrange the slices on the grill , turn the side, until the eggplant is tender. Set them aside.

2. In a small bowl, merge all the dry spices excluding salt and pepper.

3. In a frying pan, cook the spice mixture in olive oil for about 30 seconds. Add the onion and cook until translucent. Add the tomatoes, molasses, garlic and vinegar. Cook the sauce, until thickened. Season with the salt and pepper.

4. Transfer the eggplant to the serving platter, pour the cooked sauce over, and garnish with the cilantro.Serve and enjoy!

NUTRITIONAL INFORMATION PER SERVING:

Calories	103
	% Daily Value*
Total Fat 4.3g	5%
Saturated Fat 0.6g	3%
Cholesterol 0mg	0%
Sodium 157mg	7%
Total Carbohydrate 16.3g	6%
Dietary Fiber 5.7g	20%
Total Sugars 9.3g	
Protein 2.4g	
Vitamin D 0mcg	0%
Calcium 43mg	3%
Iron 1mg	6%
Potassium 591mg	13%

Easy

40 minutes

2 Servings

INGREDIENTS:

- ¼ cup black beans
- 2 cloves garlic, chopped
- 2 pinches salt
- 3 tablespoons chopped fresh cilantro
- 1 cup water
- ½ tablespoon olive oil

PREPARATION:

1. In a large over put water and black beans and boil them until tender. You may pressure cook for 30 min or let it simmer on medium low heat for 1 hour. Strain cooked beans and transfer them in a large bowl.

2. Mash beans and garlic together. Add cilantro and salt. Make small patties and refrigerate for about 1 hour.

3. In a nonstick frying pan, heat the olive oil and cook these patties. Turn the sides when the outside is slightly crisp, about 5 minutes. Serve immediately.

NUTRITIONAL INFORMATION PER SERVING:

Calories	200
	% Daily Value*
Total Fat 4.2g	5%
Saturated Fat 0.7g	3%
Cholesterol 0mg	0%
Sodium 154mg	7%
Total Carbohydrate 31.3g	11%
Dietary Fiber 7.5g	27%
Total Sugars 1.1g	
Protein 10.7g	
Vitamin D 0mcg	0%
Calcium 69mg	5%
Iron 3mg	14%
Potassium 738mg	16%

Very Easy

20 minutes

2 Servings

INGREDIENTS:

- 1½ teaspoons olive oil, divided
- ½ medium onion, thinly sliced
- 1 tablespoon water
- ½ pound fresh green beans
- ¼ teaspoon dried ground thyme
- ¾ cup skim milk
- 1/8 cup finely chopped onion
- ½ clove garlic, finely chopped
- ¼ cup fresh whole grain bread crumbs
- ¾ cup sliced mushrooms
- 1½ tablespoons all-purpose flour

PREPARATION:

1. Heat oven to 350 F.
2. In a skillet, put 2 teaspoons of olive oil and sliced onion over low heat and sauté for 3 minutes.
3. Remove onions from the skillet and set aside.
4. Add 1 teaspoon of olive oil, add chopped onion and garlic and cook for 2 to 3 minutes. Add water and mushrooms and cook for 5 min.
5. Next slowly sprinkle flour and thyme over mixture and stir thoroughly. Gradually add milk and stir constantly until the sauce thickens.
6. In a microwave safe bowl, add beans with 2 tablespoons of water, cover and microwave for 5 minutes on high. Set them aside.
7. Spray a casserole with cooking spray and place the green beans in the casserole.
8. Pour the mushroom sauce over the green beans along with sauteed onion slices and fresh bread crumbs.
9. Bake for 15 minutes and dish out to serve.

NUTRITIONAL INFORMATION PER SERVING:

Calories	74
	% Daily Value*
Total Fat 1.7g	2%
Saturated Fat 0.2g	1%
Cholesterol 1mg	0%
Sodium 45mg	2%
Total Carbohydrate 12.6g	5%
Dietary Fiber 2.6g	9%
Total Sugars 3.7g	
Protein 3.3g	
Vitamin D 38mcg	190%
Calcium 69mg	5%
Iron 1mg	7%
Potassium 221mg	5%

CRISPY POTATO WEDGES

Very Easy

20 minutes

2 Servings

INGREDIENTS:

- 2 medium potatoes
- cooking spray
- 1/8 teaspoon black pepper
- 1/8 teaspoon sea salt
- 1 tablespoon minced fresh rosemary

PREPARATION:

1. Set the oven's temperature to 375 degrees Fahrenheit.
2. Cut the potatoes in the form of wedges. wash and pierce the wedges with a fork.
3. Position gently in the oven and bake for 1 hour, or until the skins are crisp.
4. Coat the baking tray with the cooking spray.
5. In a large bowl, combine the rosemary, salt and pepper. Put the potatoes in the bowl and coat with the seasoning.
6. Bake the potatoes back in the oven for 10 minutes. Serve right away.
7. Serve and enjoy!

NUTRITIONAL INFORMATION PER SERVING:

Calories	155
	% Daily Value*
Total Fat 0.7g	1%
Saturated Fat 0.2g	1%
Cholesterol 0mg	0%
Sodium 131mg	6%
Total Carbohydrate 34.6g	13%
Dietary Fiber 5.8g	21%
Total Sugars 2.5g	
Protein 3.7g	
Vitamin D 0mcg	0%
Calcium 41mg	3%
Iron 2mg	9%
Potassium 884mg	19%

Very Easy

10 minutes

2 Servings

INGREDIENTS:

- 8 ounces chicken tenderloins
- 3 tablespoons black sesame seeds, toasted
- ¼ teaspoon coarse salt
- 1 teaspoon sesame oil
- 1 teaspoon low sodium soy sauce
- 2 tablespoons breadcrumbs
- Olive oil spray

PREPARATION:

1. Set the oven's temperature to 425 degrees F and spray the baking sheet with the cooking spray.

2. In a bowl combine the sesame seeds, salt, and bread crumbs.

3. Add oil and soya sauce in the chicken. Then coat chicken thoroughly with the sesame seed and bread crumbs mixture.

4. Place the chicken on the baking tray and spray with oil . Bake for 8-10 minutes until well done.

5. Serve and enjoy!

NUTRITIONAL INFORMATION PER SERVING:

Calories	286
	% Daily Value*
Total Fat 14g	18%
Saturated Fat 2.7g	13%
Cholesterol 80mg	27%
Sodium 1049mg	46%
Total Carbohydrate 9.6g	3%
Dietary Fiber 1.9g	7%
Total Sugars 0.5g	
Protein 31.6g	
Vitamin D 0mcg	0%
Calcium 144mg	11%
Iron 2mg	13%
Potassium 81mg	2%

MINTED BABY CARROTS

Very Easy

10 minutes

2 Servings

INGREDIENTS:

- 1½ cups baby carrots
- 3 tablespoons apple juice
- 2 cups water
- 1 pinch teaspoon ground cinnamon
- ¼ tablespoon cornstarch
- ¼ tablespoon chopped fresh mint leaves

PREPARATION:

1. In a large pan pour water and add carrots. Boil for about 10 minutes until tender- crisp. Drain the carrots well and keep aside in a bowl.

2. In a saucepan combine the apple juice and cornstarch. Stir continuously until the mixture thickens. Add mint and cinnamon.

3. Pour the mixture over the carrots. Serve and enjoy!

NUTRITIONAL INFORMATION PER SERVING:

Calories	55
	% Daily Value*
Total Fat 0.2g	0%
Saturated Fat 0g	0%
Cholesterol 0mg	0%
Sodium 100mg	4%
Total Carbohydrate 13g	5%
Dietary Fiber 3.4g	12%
Total Sugars 6.9g	
Protein 0.8g	
Vitamin D 0mcg	0%
Calcium 50mg	4%
Iron 1mg	6%
Potassium 292mg	6%

ROASTED TOMATOES

Very Easy

20 minutes

2 Servings

INGREDIENTS:

- ¾ pound cherry tomatoes – Halved
- Pinch of salt
- Black pepper, to taste
- Rosemerry strand
- 1½ tablespoon olive oil

PREPARATION:

1. Sprinkle each tomato half with the salt and pepper
2. Set aside for about 40 minutes.
3. Preheat your oven to 425 °F. Grease a baking tray and line it with parchment paper.
4. Arrange the tomato halves onto the prepared baking sheet, and drizzle with olive oil. Put rosermerry strand on top.
5. Roast for approximately 20 minutes.
6. Serve warm.

NUTRITIONAL INFORMATION PER SERVING:

Calories	110
	% Daily Value*
Total Fat 9.7g	12%
Saturated Fat 1.4g	7%
Cholesterol 0mg	0%
Sodium 59mg	3%
Total Carbohydrate 6.5g	2%
Dietary Fiber 2g	7%
Total Sugars 4.4g	
Protein 1.5g	
Vitamin D 0mcg	0%
Calcium 17mg	1%
Iron 0mg	3%
Potassium 395mg	8%

ACORN SQUASH WITH APPLES

Very Easy

10 minutes

2 Servings

INGREDIENTS:

- 1 apple, peeled, cored and sliced
- 1 acorn squash
- 2 tablespoons brown sugar
- 2 teaspoons margarine

PREPARATION:

1. In a small bowl mix apples with brown sugar and set aside.

2. Pierce squash with the fork and put it in the microwave for 5 min. Turn the squash after 3 min to ensure even cooking

3. Place the squash on the cutting board and deseed. Fill the hollow space of the squash with apple mixture

4. Put it in the microwave on a high for another 2 min until apples are softened.

5. Serve the squash with the margarine on the top. Enjoy!

NUTRITIONAL INFORMATION PER SERVING:

Calories	212
	% Daily Value*
Total Fat 4.2g	5%
Saturated Fat 0.7g	3%
Cholesterol 0mg	0%
Sodium 54mg	2%
Total Carbohydrate 46.7g	17%
Dietary Fiber 5.9g	21%
Total Sugars 20.3g	
Protein 2.1g	
Vitamin D 0mcg	0%
Calcium 81mg	6%
Iron 2mg	11%
Potassium 881mg	19%

POTATO SALAD

Very Easy

10 minutes

2 Servings

INGREDIENTS:

- ¼ pound potatoes, diced and boiled or steamed
- ¼ large yellow onion, chopped
- ¼ large carrot, diced
- ½ ribs celery, diced
- ½ tablespoon minced fresh dill
- ¼ teaspoon ground black pepper
- 3 tablespoons low-calorie mayonnaise
- ¼ tablespoon Dijon mustard
- ½ tablespoon red wine vinegar

PREPARATION:

1. Dice the potatoes and boil them.
2. Combine boiled potatoes and all the ingredients in a large mixing bowl.
3. Chill in the refrigerator
4. Serve and enjoy!!

NUTRITIONAL INFORMATION PER SERVING:

Calories	85
	% Daily Value*
Total Fat 2.7g	3%
Saturated Fat 0.4g	2%
Cholesterol 2mg	1%
Sodium 92mg	4%
Total Carbohydrate 14.2g	5%
Dietary Fiber 2.3g	8%
Total Sugars 2.5g	
Protein 1.6g	
Vitamin D 0mcg	0%
Calcium 32mg	2%
Iron 1mg	5%
Potassium 338mg	7%

STEWS AND SOUPS

PEAS AND CAULIFLOWER STEW

 Medium

 35 minutes

 2 Servings

INGREDIENTS:

- 1 large onion, chopped
- 2 tablespoons olive oil
- 2 garlic cloves, minced
- Pinch of salt
- 1½ cups peas
- 1 tablespoon fresh lemon juice
- ¼ teaspoon fresh ginger root, grated finely
- Black pepper, to taste
- 2 cups vegetable broth, salt-free
- 1½ cups small cauliflower florets

PREPARATION:

1. In a large soup pan, put olive oil and onion for about 4 minutes over medium heat.
2. Stir in the ginger and garlic and sauté for about 1 minute.
3. Add salt, black pepper, and broth and let it reach a boil.
4. Add the vegetables and boil again.
5. Cover the pan and cook for about 20 minutes, occasionally stirring.
6. Stir in the lemon juice and dish out to serve hot.

NUTRITIONAL INFORMATION PER SERVING:

Calories	107
	% Daily Value*
Total Fat 7.2g	9%
Saturated Fat 1g	5%
Cholesterol 0mg	0%
Sodium 329mg	14%
Total Carbohydrate 9.9g	4%
Dietary Fiber 3.2g	11%
Total Sugars 4.2g	
Protein 2.2g	
Vitamin D 0mcg	0%
Calcium 46mg	4%
Iron 1mg	4%
Potassium 288mg	6%

Easy

20 minutes

2 Servings

INGREDIENTS:

- 1 small cucumber, peeled, seeded, and chopped
- 2 lb. fresh strawberries, hulled and sliced
- ½ cup fresh basil leaves
- 1 pinch of salt
- ½ cup red onion, chopped
- ¼ cup balsamic vinegar
- 1 tablespoon olive oil
- ½ cup bell pepper, seeded and chopped
- 1 small jalapeño pepper, seeded and chopped

PREPARATION:

1. In a blender, merge all ingredients and blitz well.
2. Ladle out into a large bowl and cover it with a wrap.
3. Refrigerate for sometime before serving.

NUTRITIONAL INFORMATION PER SERVING:

Calories	579
	% Daily Value*
Total Fat 21.9g	28%
Saturated Fat 2.7g	13%
Cholesterol 62mg	21%
Sodium 1096mg	48%
Total Carbohydrate 62.8g	23%
Dietary Fiber 16.5g	59%
Total Sugars 13.7g	
Protein 35.6g	
Vitamin D 0mcg	0%
Calcium 171mg	13%
Iron 7mg	38%
Potassium 1670mg	36%

CHICKEN AND BROCCOLI STEW

Easy

28 minutes

2 Servings

INGREDIENTS:

- 7 oz. chicken breasts, cut into small pieces, boneless, skinless
- 1 tablespoon olive oil
- ½ large onion, chopped
- 1 cup broccoli
- Pinch of salt
- ¾ cup tomatoes, chopped finely
- ¾ cup water
- Ground black pepper, to taste

PREPARATION:

1. In a soup pan, put the oil, chicken pieces, and onion, and cook for about 5 minutes.
2. Add the tomatoes and cook for about 3 minutes.
3. Add the broccoli, water, salt and black pepper and cook for about 20 minutes.
4. Ladle out in a bowl and serve hot.

NUTRITIONAL INFORMATION PER SERVING:

Calories	368
	% Daily Value*
Total Fat 15g	19%
Saturated Fat 3.1g	16%
Cholesterol 88mg	29%
Sodium 135mg	6%
Total Carbohydrate 22.5g	8%
Dietary Fiber 7.4g	26%
Total Sugars 9.8g	
Protein 35.9g	
Vitamin D 0mcg	0%
Calcium 59mg	5%
Iron 3mg	17%
Potassium 733mg	16%

SPINACH AND BEANS SOUP

Easy

30 minutes

2 Servings

INGREDIENTS:

- ½ onions, chopped
- ½ tablespoons olive oil
- 1 garlic clove, minced
- 1 cup cooked cannellini beans
- Pinch of salt
- ¼ lb. kale, tough ribs removed and chopped
- 2 cups water
- Ground black pepper, to taste

PREPARATION:

1. In a large pan, sauté onion and garlic in the oil over medium heat for about 5 minutes.
2. Add the kale and cook for about 2 minutes.
3. Stir in the beans, water, salt, and black pepper and let it come to a boil.
4. Cover the lid partially and cook for about 20 minutes.
5. Ladle out in a bowl and serve hot.

NUTRITIONAL INFORMATION PER SERVING:

Calories	503
	% Daily Value*
Total Fat 5.7g	7%
Saturated Fat 0.8g	4%
Cholesterol 0mg	0%
Sodium 98mg	4%
Total Carbohydrate 85.6g	31%
Dietary Fiber 32.5g	116%
Total Sugars 4.3g	
Protein 31.7g	
Vitamin D 0mcg	0%
Calcium 296mg	23%
Iron 11mg	63%
Potassium 2160mg	46%

CHICKPEAS AND VEGETABLE STEW

Easy

35 minutes

2 Servings

INGREDIENTS:

- 2 cups water
- ¾ cup portabella mushrooms, chopped
- ½ cup cooked chickpeas
- ½ cup white onion, chopped
- ½ cup butternut squash, peeled, seeded and chopped
- 1 tablespoon olive oil
- Ground black pepper, to taste
- ½ cup fresh kale, tough ribs removed and chopped
- ½ cup bell peppers, seeded and chopped
- 1 tomato, chopped
- ½ teaspoon mixed dried herbs

PREPARATION:

1. In a large soup pan, merge chicken with all other ingredients and let it come to a rolling boil.
2. Switch the heat to low and simmer, covered for about 1 hour, occasionally stirring.
3. Ladle out in a bowl and serve hot.

NUTRITIONAL INFORMATION PER SERVING:

Calories	337
	% Daily Value*
Total Fat 10.4g	13%
Saturated Fat 1.4g	7%
Cholesterol 0mg	0%
Sodium 123mg	5%
Total Carbohydrate 51g	19%
Dietary Fiber 12.3g	44%
Total Sugars 11.7g	
Protein 14.1g	
Vitamin D 0mcg	0%
Calcium 111mg	9%
Iron 5mg	26%
Potassium 1140mg	24%

CUCUMBER SOUP

Medium

40 minutes

2 Servings

INGREDIENTS:

- ¾ pound cucumbers, trimmed and chopped
- ½ tablespoon olive oil
- 2 scallions, chopped
- 1 tablespoon fresh lemon juice
- 2 cups low-sodium vegetable broth
- ½ Serrano pepper, seeded and chopped finely

PREPARATION:

1. In a large frying-pan, put the olive oil and scallions and cook for about 5 minutes over medium heat.
2. Add cucumber and broth and let it come to a boil.
3. Switch the heat to low and simmer, covered for about 30 minutes, occasionally stirring.
4. Eliminate the pan from the heat and move to the food processor.
5. Pulse well until smooth mixture is formed and return it into the pan.
6. Cook for about 5 minutes over medium-heat and squeeze in the lemon juice.
7. Dust with salt and black pepper and eliminate from the heat.
8. Ladle out in a bowl and serve hot.

NUTRITIONAL INFORMATION PER SERVING:

Calories	86
% Daily Value*	
Total Fat 3.8g	5%
Saturated Fat 0.6g	3%
Cholesterol 0mg	0%
Sodium 78mg	3%
Total Carbohydrate 9g	3%
Dietary Fiber 4.1g	14%
Total Sugars 3.8g	
Protein 6.1g	
Vitamin D 0mcg	0%
Calcium 52mg	4%
Iron 4mg	24%
Potassium 399mg	8%

LENTIL, VEGGIE AND BARLEY STEW

Easy

50 minutes

2 Servings

INGREDIENTS:

- ¼ carrot, peeled and chopped
- ¼ tablespoon olive oil
- ¼ red onion, chopped
- ¼ garlic cloves, minced
- ¼ cup red lentils
- 2 cups salt-free vegetable broth
- Pinch of salt
- ½ celery stalk, chopped
- ¼ cup barley
- 1½ cups tomatoes, chopped finely
- 2 cups fresh spinach, torn
- Ground black pepper, as required

PREPARATION:

1. In a large pan, put the oil, carrots, onion, and celery and sauté for about 5 minutes over medium heat.
2. Add garlic and sauté for about 1 minute.
3. Stir in the barley, lentils, tomatoes, and broth and let it reach a rolling boil.
4. Switch the heat to low, cover the lid and simmer for about 40 minutes.
5. Stir in the spinach, salt and black pepper and simmer for about 4 minutes.
6. Dish out and serve hot.

NUTRITIONAL INFORMATION PER SERVING:

Calories	248
	% Daily Value*
Total Fat 4.6g	6%
Saturated Fat 0.7g	3%
Cholesterol 0mg	0%
Sodium 459mg	20%
Total Carbohydrate 42.4g	15%
Dietary Fiber 14.8g	53%
Total Sugars 6.8g	
Protein 11.1g	
Vitamin D 0mcg	0%
Calcium 82mg	6%
Iron 4mg	22%
Potassium 816mg	17%

KALE AND DANDELION GREENS SOUP

Easy

15 minutes

1 Servings

INGREDIENTS:

- 1½ cups fresh watercress
- 1½ cups fresh kale, tough ribs removed and chopped
- 1½ cups dandelion greens
- 1½ cups water
- ¾ tablespoon fresh lime juice
- Pinch of salt
- 1½ garlic cloves, peeled
- ¾ cup unsweetened coconut milk
- ½ teaspoon cayenne powder

PREPARATION:

1. In a high-powered blender, merge all the soup ingredients and pulse on high speed until smooth.
2. Move the soup into a pan over medium heat and cook for about 5 minutes.
3. Ladle out in a bowl and serve hot.

NUTRITIONAL INFORMATION PER SERVING:

Calories	235
	% Daily Value*
Total Fat 19.5g	25%
Saturated Fat 17g	85%
Cholesterol 0mg	0%
Sodium 129mg	6%
Total Carbohydrate 14.6g	5%
Dietary Fiber 4.2g	15%
Total Sugars 3.3g	
Protein 5.1g	
Vitamin D 0mcg	0%
Calcium 159mg	12%
Iron 3mg	19%
Potassium 650mg	14%

RED BEANS STEW

Medium

30 minutes

2 Servings

INGREDIENTS:

- ½ tablespoon olive oil
- 1 small onion, chopped
- 2½ garlic cloves, finely chopped
- ½ teaspoon ground cumin
- ½ teaspoon dried oregano
- ½ cup vegetable broth, salt-free
- Black pepper, to taste
- 2 cups red beans, cooked
- Pinch of salt
- 1 cup tomatoes, chopped

PREPARATION:

1. In a pan, put the olive oil and onions and cook for about 7 minutes over medium heat, stirring frequently.
2. Add garlic, oregano, cumin, salt, and black pepper and cook for about 1 minute.
3. Add the tomatoes and cook for about 2 minutes.
4. Stir in the red beans and broth and let it come to a boil.
5. Switch the heat to medium-low and simmer, covered for about 15 minutes.
6. Ladle out in a bowl and serve hot.

NUTRITIONAL INFORMATION PER SERVING:

Calories	592
	% Daily Value*
Total Fat 5.6g	7%
Saturated Fat 1.1g	5%
Cholesterol 0mg	0%
Sodium 197mg	9%
Total Carbohydrate 103.8g	38%
Dietary Fiber 25.3g	90%
Total Sugars 6.6g	
Protein 35.7g	
Vitamin D 0mcg	0%
Calcium 221mg	17%
Iron 9mg	48%
Potassium 2579mg	55%

MAHI MAHI AND VEGGIE SOUP

Medium

35 minutes

2 Servings

INGREDIENTS:

- ¼ Jalapeno pepper, chopped
- ½ boneless Mahi Mahi fillets, cubed
- ¼ shallot, chopped
- ½ small bell pepper, seeded and chopped
- ½ tablespoon fresh lemon juice
- ½ garlic clove, minced
- 1½ cups vegetable broth, low-sodium
- 1 tablespoon fresh cilantro, minced
- ½ tablespoon olive oil
- ¼ head Chinese cabbage, chopped
- Fresh ground black pepper, to taste

PREPARATION:

1. In a large soup pan, put olive oil, shallot, and garlic, and cook for about 3 minutes over medium heat.
2. Stir in the cabbage and bell peppers and cook for about 4 minutes.
3. Add broth and thoroughly boil over high heat.
4. Switch the heat to medium-low and gently cook for about 10 minutes.
5. Add Mahi Mahi and cook for about 6 minutes.
6. Stir in the cilantro, lemon juice, and black pepper and cook for about 2 minutes.
7. Ladle out in a bowl and serve hot!

NUTRITIONAL INFORMATION PER SERVING:

Calories	144
	% Daily Value*
Total Fat 7.6g	10%
Saturated Fat 1.2g	6%
Cholesterol 20mg	7%
Sodium 662mg	29%
Total Carbohydrate 5.9g	2%
Dietary Fiber 1.6g	6%
Total Sugars 3.4g	
Protein 14.3g	
Vitamin D 0mcg	0%
Calcium 138mg	11%
Iron 2mg	9%
Potassium 665mg	14%

VEGETARIAN

VEGGIE HUMMUS SANDWICH

Easy   10 minutes   2 Servings

INGREDIENTS:

- 6 tablespoons hummus
- 4 slices whole grain bread
- ½ avocado, mashed
- ½ medium red bell pepper, sliced
- ½ cup carrots, shredded
- 1 cup mixed salad greens
- ½ cup cucumber, sliced

PREPARATION:

1. Layer one slice of bread with hummus and other with avocado.
2. Top with greens, bell pepper, cucumber, and carrot.
3. Slice in half before serving.

NUTRITIONAL INFORMATION PER SERVING:

Calories	256
% Daily Value*	
Total Fat 14.6g	19%
Saturated Fat 2.8g	14%
Cholesterol 0mg	0%
Sodium 323mg	14%
Total Carbohydrate 27.6g	10%
Dietary Fiber 7.5g	27%
Total Sugars 4.3g	
Protein 7.2g	
Vitamin D 0mcg	0%
Calcium 74mg	6%
Iron 3mg	15%
Potassium 659mg	14%

PICKLED BEETS

Very Easy

10 minutes

2 Servings

INGREDIENTS:

- 4 tablespoons pearl onions, trimmed
- ¼ pound fresh beets, chopped
- 4 tablespoons white wine vinegar
- ¼ sprig fresh dill
- 3 whole black peppercorns
- 2 whole coriander seeds
- 3 tablespoons cider vinegar
- ¼ cup water
- 1 clove garlic, whole
- 2 pinches red pepper flakes

PREPARATION:

1. Merge all the ingredients in airtight containers.
2. Refrigerate for up to 1 month before serving.
3. Serve and enjoy!

NUTRITIONAL INFORMATION PER SERVING:

Calories	17
	% Daily Value*
Total Fat 0.2g	0%
Saturated Fat 0g	0%
Cholesterol 0mg	0%
Sodium 5mg	0%
Total Carbohydrate 2.9g	1%
Dietary Fiber 1.3g	5%
Total Sugars 1.1g	
Protein 1.2g	
Vitamin D 0mcg	0%
Calcium 21mg	2%
Iron 1mg	7%
Potassium 131mg	3%

Gnocchi Pomodoro

Medium

30 minutes

2 Servings

INGREDIENTS:

- ½ medium onion, finely chopped
- 1½ tablespoons extra-virgin olive oil, divided
- 1 large clove garlic, minced
- ¾ cup no-salt-added whole tomatoes, pulsed in a food processor until chunky
- ½ tablespoon butter
- ½ package gnocchi
- 2 pinches red pepper, crushed
- 2 pinches salt
- 3 tablespoons fresh basil, chopped
- Grated Parmesan cheese, for garnish

PREPARATION:

1. In a large skillet, sauté onions in 2 tablespoons of oil for about 5 minutes over medium heat.
2. Add garlic and crushed red pepper and cook for about 1 minute.
3. Add tomatoes and salt and let it come to a simmer.
4. Switch the heat to low and cook for about 20 minutes, frequently stirring.
5. Eliminate the pan from the heat and stir in butter and basil.
6. In a large nonstick skillet, put the remaining 1 tablespoon oil over medium-high heat.
7. Cook for about 7 minutes, frequently tossing.
8. Stir the gnocchi into the tomato sauce and dish out to serve.

NUTRITIONAL INFORMATION PER SERVING:

Calories	236
% Daily Value*	
Total Fat 14.3g	18%
Saturated Fat 3.6g	18%
Cholesterol 9mg	3%
Sodium 527mg	23%
Total Carbohydrate 24.1g	9%
Dietary Fiber 3g	11%
Total Sugars 2.7g	
Protein 3.7g	
Vitamin D 2mcg	10%
Calcium 59mg	5%
Iron 1mg	3%
Potassium 164mg	3%

PEA & SPINACH CARBONARA

Medium

50 minutes

4 Servings

INGREDIENTS:

- 1½ tablespoons olive oil, extra-virgin
- 1 garlic clove, minced
- 3 tablespoons fresh parsley, finely chopped
- 1 large egg
- ¼ teaspoon salt
- 8 cups baby spinach
- ½ cup panko breadcrumbs, whole-wheat
- 8 tablespoons Parmesan cheese, grated and divided
- 3 large egg yolks
- ½ teaspoon ground pepper
- 1 (9 ounce) package fresh linguine
- 1 cup peas

PREPARATION:

1. In a large skillet, put breadcrumbs and garlic in oil and cook for about 2 minutes.
2. Dish out in a bowl add add parsley and 2 tbsp parmesan.
3. In a bowl, merge remaining parmesan with egg, pepper, egg yolks, and salt.
4. Add pasta in boiling water and cook for 1 minute.
5. Stir in the peas and spinach and cook for 1 more minute.
6. Drain well and reserve ¼ cup boiled water.
7. Slowly put reserved water into the egg mixture.
8. Whisk in this mixture inside the pasta and serve topped with breadcrumb mixture.

NUTRITIONAL INFORMATION PER SERVING:

Calories	413
% Daily Value*	
Total Fat 15g	19%
Saturated Fat 4.6g	23%
Cholesterol 260mg	87%
Sodium 380mg	17%
Total Carbohydrate 51g	19%
Dietary Fiber 4.4g	16%
Total Sugars 2.8g	
Protein 20.6g	
Vitamin D 18mcg	90%
Calcium 233mg	18%
Iron 6mg	31%
Potassium 590mg	13%

STUFFED SWEET POTATO WITH HUMMUS DRESSING

Medium

20 minutes

2 Servings

INGREDIENTS:

- ½ large sweet potato, scrubbed
- ½ cups canned black beans, rinsed
- 1 tablespoon water
- ½ cup chopped kale
- 1/8 cup hummus

PREPARATION:

1. Prick the entire sweet potato and microwave for 10 minutes on high.
2. In a medium saucepan, put the kale and cook over medium-high heat, stirring twice.
3. Add the beans and 2 tablespoons of water, and cook for about 2 minutes, stirring regularly.
4. Cut open the sweet potato and stuff with the kale and bean mixture.
5. In a small bowl, merge hummus and 2 tablespoons of water.
6. Trickle the hummus dressing over the stuffed sweet potatoes and serve.

NUTRITIONAL INFORMATION PER SERVING:

Calories	191
	% Daily Value*
Total Fat 1.8g	2%
Saturated Fat 0.3g	2%
Cholesterol 0mg	0%
Sodium 67mg	3%
Total Carbohydrate 34.5g	13%
Dietary Fiber 8g	29%
Total Sugars 3.2g	
Protein 10.4g	
Vitamin D 0mcg	0%
Calcium 67mg	5%
Iron 4mg	20%
Potassium 824mg	18%

PEA & SPINACH CARBONARA

Easy

23 minutes

2 Servings

INGREDIENTS:

- 1 garlic clove, chopped
- 1 tablespoon olive oil
- 1 cup tomatoes, chopped
- ½ teaspoon fresh ginger root, chopped
- ½ teaspoon curry powder, salt-free
- 1/8 teaspoon red chili powder
- ¾ cup water
- Ground black pepper, to taste
- ¼ teaspoon ground cumin
- 2 cups tofu
- 1/8 cup coconut milk, unsweetened

PREPARATION:

1. In a food processor, merge tomatoes, garlic, and ginger and pulse until smooth.
2. In a pan, put the oil, curry powder and spices and sauté for about 1 minute over medium heat.
3. Add the tomato mixture and cook for about 5 minutes.
4. Stir in the tofu, water, and coconut milk and let it come to a boil.
5. Cook for about 12 minutes, occasionally stirring.
6. Dust with black pepper and serve hot.

NUTRITIONAL INFORMATION PER SERVING:

Calories	105
% Daily Value*	
Total Fat 8.9g	11%
Saturated Fat 3.4g	17%
Cholesterol 0mg	0%
Sodium 15mg	1%
Total Carbohydrate 6.2g	2%
Dietary Fiber 1.9g	7%
Total Sugars 3.3g	
Protein 2.9g	
Vitamin D 202mcg	1008%
Calcium 20mg	2%
Iron 2mg	13%
Potassium 400mg	9%

OKRA CURRY

Easy

12 minutes

2 Servings

INGREDIENTS:

- 2 garlic cloves, minced
- 1 tablespoon olive oil
- ¼ teaspoon red pepper flakes, crushed
- Ground black pepper, as required
- ½ lb. asparagus, trimmed and cut into 1½-inch pieces
- Pinch of salt
- ¼ lb. cooked whole-wheat pasta, drained

PREPARATION:

1. In a non-stick wok, sauté garlic, red pepper flakes, and hot pepper sauce in the oil for about 1 minute over medium heat.
2. Add the asparagus, salt, and black pepper and cook for about 10 minutes, occasionally stirring.
3. Place the hot pasta and toss to coat well.
4. Dish out and serve immediately.

NUTRITIONAL INFORMATION PER SERVING:

Calories	302
	% Daily Value*
Total Fat 8.3g	11%
Saturated Fat 1.1g	5%
Cholesterol 0mg	0%
Sodium 47mg	2%
Total Carbohydrate 48.3g	18%
Dietary Fiber 4.6g	16%
Total Sugars 2.2g	
Protein 10.9g	
Vitamin D 0mcg	0%
Calcium 35mg	3%
Iron 3mg	14%
Potassium 249mg	5%

QUINOA WITH VEGGIES

Easy

15 minutes

2 Servings

INGREDIENTS:

- ½ small white onion, chopped
- 1 tablespoon olive oil
- ¼ cup frozen green peas, thawed
- 1/8 cup frozen corn, thawed
- 2½ tablespoons soy sauce, low-sodium
- ¼ cup frozen carrots, thawed
- 1½ cups quinoa, cooked
- 1½ tablespoons scallions, chopped

PREPARATION:

1. In a large-sized non-stick wok, put the oil and onion and sauté for about 4-5 minutes over medium heat.
2. Add the peas, carrot, and corn and cook for about 4 minutes.
3. Stir in the remaining ingredients and cook for about 3 minutes.
4. Dish out and serve hot.

NUTRITIONAL INFORMATION PER SERVING:

Calories	456
	% Daily Value*
Total Fat 11.9g	15%
Saturated Fat 1.6g	8%
Cholesterol 0mg	0%
Sodium 379mg	16%
Total Carbohydrate 72.2g	26%
Dietary Fiber 8.9g	32%
Total Sugars 2.6g	
Protein 16.2g	
Vitamin D 0mcg	0%
Calcium 61mg	5%
Iron 5mg	29%
Potassium 678mg	14%

CHICKPEAS WITH SWISS CHARD

Easy

15 minutes

2 Servings

INGREDIENTS:

- ½ garlic clove, sliced thinly
- ½ tablespoon olive oil
- ¼ tomato, chopped finely
- 1 cup cooked chickpeas
- 1/8 cup water
- ½ bunches fresh Swiss chard, trimmed
- Ground black pepper, as required
- ¼ tablespoon fresh lemon juice

PREPARATION:

1. In a large wok, put the oil and garlic and sauté for about 1 minute over medium heat.
2. Add the tomato and cook for about 3 minutes, crushing well.
3. Stir in rest of the ingredients excluding lemon juice and parsley and cook for about 7 minutes.
4. Squeeze in the lemon juice and dish out to serve hot.

NUTRITIONAL INFORMATION PER SERVING:

Calories	354
% Daily Value*	
Total Fat 9.8g	13%
Saturated Fat 1.2g	6%
Cholesterol 0mg	0%
Sodium 57mg	2%
Total Carbohydrate 52.7g	19%
Dietary Fiber 15.2g	54%
Total Sugars 10g	
Protein 16.7g	
Vitamin D 0mcg	0%
Calcium 101mg	8%
Iron 6mg	31%
Potassium 869mg	18%

Condiment, Broth, and Seasoning

Cajun Spice Mix

Very Easy

5 minutes

¼ cup

INGREDIENTS:

- 2 teaspoons white pepper
- 2 teaspoons garlic powder
- 2 teaspoons onion powder
- 2 teaspoons of cayenne pepper
- 2 teaspoons paprika
- 2 teaspoons of ground black pepper

PREPARATION:

1. Mix all the ingredients through a food processor to get a fine texture. Put it in a container with an airtight lid. Store for 4 weeks.
2. It can be used on meats, vegetables and casseroles.

NUTRITIONAL INFORMATION PER SERVING:

Calories	10
	% Daily Value*
Total Fat 0.2g	0%
Saturated Fat 0g	0%
Cholesterol 0mg	0%
Sodium 1mg	0%
Total Carbohydrate 2.2g	1%
Dietary Fiber 0.7g	3%
Total Sugars 0.5g	
Protein 0.4g	
Vitamin D 0mcg	0%
Calcium 9mg	1%
Iron 1mg	3%
Potassium 48mg	1%

HOMEMADE FAJITA SEASONING MIX

Very Easy

5 minutes

1/3 cup

INGREDIENTS:

- 2 teaspoon of red chili powder
- 2 teaspoon ground cumin
- ¼ teaspoon of Sea salt
- 2 teaspoon of oregano
- Ground black pepper
- 2 teaspoon paprika
- 2 teaspoon garlic powder
- 2 teaspoon onion powder
- 2 teaspoon dried parsley

PREPARATION:

1. Combine all the ingredients and store in the container for upto 4 weeks.

NUTRITIONAL INFORMATION PER SERVING:

Calories		11
	% Daily Value*	
Total Fat 0.3g		0%
Saturated Fat 0.1g		0%
Cholesterol 0mg		0%
Sodium 67mg		3%
Total Carbohydrate 2g		1%
Dietary Fiber 0.6g		2%
Total Sugars 0.5g		
Protein 0.5g		
Vitamin D 0mcg		0%
Calcium 16mg		1%
Iron 1mg		4%
Potassium 48mg		1%

EASY VEGETABLE STOCK

Easy

30 minutes

2 Servings

INGREDIENTS:

- 1 teaspoon olive oil
- ¼ onion, cut into 1-inch pieces
- 4 fresh white mushrooms, brushed
- clean and coarsely chopped
- ½ celery stalk with leaves, cut into
- 1-inch pieces
- 1 large carrot, cut into 1-inch pieces
- 2 cloves garlic, halved
- 2 fresh flat-leaf (Italian) parsley sprigs
- 1½ fresh thyme sprigs
- 2½ cups water
- ¼ bay leaf
- 2 pinches salt

PREPARATION:

1. In a large pan, sauté mushrooms in 2 teaspoons of olive oil over medium-high heat. Add carrots, onion, celery and garlic and saute until the vegetables turn brown.

2. Next add water, bay leaf, 0parsley, thyme and salt. Let it reach a boil and then switch the heat to low and simmer for 25-30 minutes.

3. Remove from the heat and allow to gently cool. Pour the stock through a sieve and into a bowl.

4. It can be used immediately or refrigerate for up to 3 days. Furthermore it can be stored in the freezer for later use. Yields about 6 cups.

NUTRITIONAL INFORMATION PER SERVING:

Calories	62	
% Daily Value*		
Total Fat 2.6g	3%	
Saturated Fat 0.4g	2%	
Cholesterol 0mg	0%	
Sodium 100mg	4%	
Total Carbohydrate 9g	3%	
Dietary Fiber 2.4g	8%	
Total Sugars 3.7g		
Protein 2.1g		
Vitamin D 130mcg	648%	
Calcium 53mg	4%	
Iron 2mg	12%	
Potassium 327mg	7%	

LOW SODIUM CHICKEN STOCK

Medium

120 minutes

2 Servings

INGREDIENTS:

- ½ pound bones from cooked chicken, trimmed of fat
- ½ carrot, cut into 2-inch pieces
- 1 peppercorn
- ½ celery stalk, cut into 2-inch pieces
- ½ cup chopped yellow onion
- 1 parsley sprig
- 1½ quarts cold water

PREPARATION:

1. Preheat oven at 450 F. Wash chicken bones in cold water and place them on the baking tray and roast for about 20 minutes.

2. Add the carrots, celery and onion on the same baking tray and roast bones and vegetables for another 20 minutes or until they are browned.

3. Now transfer the vegetables and bones to a large pot. Add water, peppercorns and parsley in the pot.

4. On the medium heat, slowly let it reach a boil then switch the heat to low. Cover the pot partially and simmer for 1½ hours. Eliminate from the heat and let it cool a bit.

5. Using a colander, pour the stock into a bowl. Discard the bones and solids. Let it cool at room temperature for an hour.

6. Cover and refrigerate the stock overnight. Strain the stock again to discard the solidified fat. The stock is ready to serve.

7. Can be frozen for up to 3 months. Makes about 12 cups.

NUTRITIONAL INFORMATION PER SERVING:

Calories		12
	% Daily Value*	
Total Fat 0g		0%
Saturated Fat 0g		0%
Cholesterol 0mg		0%
Sodium 24mg		1%
Total Carbohydrate 2.8g		1%
Dietary Fiber 0.7g		3%
Total Sugars 1.3g		
Protein 0.3g		
Vitamin D 0mcg		0%
Calcium 20mg		2%
Iron 0mg		1%
Potassium 81mg		2%

HERB BLEND

Very Easy

5 minutes

1/3 cup

INGREDIENTS:

- 5 teaspoons onion powder
- 2 ½ teaspoons garlic powder
- 2 ½ teaspoons sweet paprika
- 2 ½ teaspoons dry mustard
- 1 ½ teaspoons thyme
- 1 teaspoon black pepper
- ¼ teaspoon celery seed
- 1 teaspoon cayenne pepper

PREPARATION:

1. Combine all the ingredients and mix well together. Put them in a shaker and use it on salads, soups and meats.

NUTRITIONAL INFORMATION PER SERVING:

Calories	10
% Daily Value*	
Total Fat 0.3g	0%
Saturated Fat 0g	0%
Cholesterol 0mg	0%
Sodium 1mg	0%
Total Carbohydrate 1.9g	1%
Dietary Fiber 0.5g	2%
Total Sugars 0.6g	
Protein 0.5g	
Vitamin D 0mcg	0%
Calcium 12mg	1%
Iron 0mg	2%
Potassium 35mg	1%

AVOCADO DIP

Very Easy

30 minutes

2 Servings

INGREDIENTS:

- 1/8 cup fat-free sour cream
- ½ teaspoons chopped onion
- 1/8 teaspoon hot sauce
- ¼ ripe avocado, peeled, pitted and mashed (about ½ cup)

PREPARATION:

1. In a bowl, combine sour cream, hot sauce, avocado and onion. Blend ingredients evenly.
2. Serve with baked tortilla chips or raw vegetables.

NUTRITIONAL INFORMATION PER SERVING:

Calories	107

	% Daily Value*
Total Fat 7.8g	10%
Saturated Fat 1.7g	8%
Cholesterol 2mg	1%
Sodium 26mg	1%
Total Carbohydrate 7.6g	3%
Dietary Fiber 2.7g	10%
Total Sugars 1.9g	
Protein 1.6g	
Vitamin D 0mcg	0%
Calcium 37mg	3%
Iron 0mg	1%
Potassium 197mg	4%

Medium

50 minutes

2 Servings

INGREDIENTS:

- ¼ pound boneless lean beef cubes
- ½ tablespoon olive oil or canola oil
- ¼ fennel bulb, trimmed and thinly sliced
- 1¼ large shallots, chopped
- ¼ teaspoon ground black pepper (divided)
- 1¼ cup no-salt-added vegetable broth
- ¼ bay leaf
- 2 large carrots, peeled and cut into 1-inch chunks
- 6 bulbs of shallots
- 1¼ large potatoes, peeled and cut into 1-inch chunks
- 1 fresh thyme sprig
- 1 tablespoon all-purpose flour
- 1 portobello mushroom, cut into 1-inch chunks
- ¼ cup finely chopped fresh parsley

PREPARATION:

1. Dust flour on the beef cubes. In a large saucepan, put the olive oil over medium heat and add beef.
2. Cook for about 5 minutes until its colour is changed. Dish out the beef from the pan and set aside.
3. In the same pan add the fennel and shallots and saute on medium heat until softened and lightly golden; it will take 7 to 8 minutes.
4. Add ¼ teaspoon pepper, thyme and bay leaf. Sauté for 1 minute.
5. Add beef and vegetable stock. Let it reach a boil and then switch the heat to low.
6. Cover the pan and let it simmer until the meat is tender. It will take 40-45 min.
7. Next add the carrots, potatoes, onions and mushrooms. Do not add any more water.
8. Add bay leave and let the vegetable simmer for 10 more minutes. Add parsley and remaining ½ teaspoon pepper.
9. Ladle into serving bowls and serve immediately.

NUTRITIONAL INFORMATION PER SERVING:

Calories	216
% Daily Value*	
Total Fat 6.4g	8%
Saturated Fat 1.6g	8%
Cholesterol 23mg	8%
Sodium 58mg	3%
Total Carbohydrate 26.7g	10%
Dietary Fiber 4.5g	16%
Total Sugars 2.9g	
Protein 13.6g	
Vitamin D 0mcg	0%
Calcium 41mg	3%
Iron 3mg	16%
Potassium 833mg	18%

ARTICHOKE DIP

Very Easy

30 minutes

2 Servings

INGREDIENTS:

- ¼ can (15.5 ounces) artichoke hearts.
- ½ clove garlic, minced
- 1 cup chopped raw spinach
- ¼ cup cooked unsalted white beans
- 1/3 teaspoon dried thyme
- 1 teaspoon dried parsley
- ¼ teaspoon ground black pepper
- 1/8 cup low-fat sour cream
- ½ tablespoons grated Parmesan cheese

PREPARATION:

1. Preheat oven at 350 degrees Fahrenheit.
2. Drain artichokes water. In a large mixing bowl, merge all the ingredients.
3. Transfer to a heatproof glass and bake at 350 F for 30 minutes.
4. Serve this dip with raw vegetables or whole crackers.

NUTRITIONAL INFORMATION PER SERVING:

Calories	100
	% Daily Value*
Total Fat 4.7g	6%
Saturated Fat 2.9g	15%
Cholesterol 11mg	4%
Sodium 105mg	5%
Total Carbohydrate 9.7g	4%
Dietary Fiber 3g	11%
Total Sugars 0.4g	
Protein 6.1g	
Vitamin D 0mcg	0%
Calcium 129mg	10%
Iron 2mg	10%
Potassium 315mg	7%

DESSERTS

MANGO BANANA SOFT SERVE

Very Easy

10 minutes

2 Servings

INGREDIENTS:

- ¼ ripe banana
- ¼ (16-ounce) package of frozen mango chunks
- ¼ tablespoon canned light coconut milk
- ¼ tablespoon stevia
- ¼ tablespoon lime juice

PREPARATION:

1. Peel and cut banana in half. Freeze it for couple of hours until solid in a sealed freezer bag.

2. Combine the mango and stevia in a large mixing bowl and set aside for 5 minutes.

3. Blend together mango, banana, lime juice, and coconut milk for 3 to 4 minutes, until the mixture is thick and smooth.

4. Scoop out the soft serve into bowls and serve immediately for a smoother texture, or freeze until ready to do for a firmer texture.

5. Use fresh mango chunks for topping

6. Serve and enjoy!

NUTRITIONAL INFORMATION PER SERVING:

Calories	76
	% Daily Value*
Total Fat 1.3g	2%
Saturated Fat 0.9g	4%
Cholesterol 0mg	0%
Sodium 2mg	0%
Total Carbohydrate 17.3g	6%
Dietary Fiber 1.9g	7%
Total Sugars 13.4g	
Protein 1g	
Vitamin D 0mcg	0%
Calcium 11mg	1%
Iron 0mg	1%
Potassium 227mg	5%

BANANA BERRY ICE CREAM

Easy

10 minutes

2 Servings

INGREDIENTS:

- ½ cup frozen berries
- 1½ large bananas
- ¾ teaspoon vanilla extract
- ¼ cup non-fat milk

PREPARATION:

1. Peel and cut bananas into 1 inch pieces. Freeze them for couple of hours in the freezer until hard.
2. Place frozen bananas, milk and vanilla in a food processor. Process for 1-2 minutes.
3. Continue to process and keep scraping the sides, until the mixture has the soft serve ice cream consistency.
4. Add berries in the mixture and pulse until they are broken up and mixed all together.
5. Serve and enjoy!

NUTRITIONAL INFORMATION PER SERVING:

Calories		127
		% Daily Value*
Total Fat 0.5g		1%
Saturated Fat 0.1g		1%
Cholesterol 1mg		0%
Sodium 17mg		1%
Total Carbohydrate 29.3g		11%
Dietary Fiber 3.9g		14%
Total Sugars 16.7g		
Protein 2.4g		
Vitamin D 0mcg		1%
Calcium 48mg		4%
Iron 0mg		3%
Potassium 460mg		10%

VANILLA CHIA SEED PUDDING WITH TOPPINGS

Very Easy

10 minutes

2 Servings

INGREDIENTS:

- ¼ cup vanilla Greek yogurt
- 3 tablespoons chia seeds
- ¼ cup reduced-fat 2 % milk
- 4 drops vanilla extract
- ¼ tablespoon maple syrup
- Pinch salt

PREPARATION:

1. In a large bowl whisk yoghurt, milk, maple syrup, vanilla, , chia seeds and salt until well combined.
2. Cover and refrigerate for 3 to 4 hours or overnight.
3. Fill dessert in the bowls or glasses .
4. Serve chilled and enjoy!

NUTRITIONAL INFORMATION PER SERVING:

Calories	68
	% Daily Value*
Total Fat 3g	4%
Saturated Fat 0.8g	4%
Cholesterol 5mg	2%
Sodium 48mg	2%
Total Carbohydrate 7.5g	3%
Dietary Fiber 2g	7%
Total Sugars 4.7g	
Protein 4.6g	
Vitamin D 0mcg	0%
Calcium 129mg	10%
Iron 1mg	3%
Potassium 66mg	1%

STRAWBERRY SOUFFLE

Medium

15 minutes

2 Servings

INGREDIENTS:

- 6 oz. fresh strawberries, hulled
- 1/8 cup unsweetened applesauce divided
- 2 egg whites, divided
- 1¼ teaspoons fresh lemon juice

PREPARATION:

1. Preheat your oven to 350 °F.
2. Puree strawberries in a blender.
3. In a bowl strain the strawberry puree through a sieve and discard the seeds.
4. Add apple sauce and lemon juice in the puree and set aside.
5. Beat egg whites in a speperate bowl until stiff peaks are formed.
6. Add some of the egg whites and fold them in the strawberry puree so that it becomes light in texture. Gently fold all the egg whites into strawberry mixture.
7. Transfer the mixture into 6 large ramekins.
8. Arrange the ramekins onto a baking sheet and bake for approximately 10-12 minutes.
9. Serve warm.

NUTRITIONAL INFORMATION PER SERVING:

Calories	48
% Daily Value*	
Total Fat 0.4g	0%
Saturated Fat 0g	0%
Cholesterol 0mg	0%
Sodium 29mg	1%
Total Carbohydrate 8.3g	3%
Dietary Fiber 1.9g	7%
Total Sugars 5.8g	
Protein 3.6g	
Vitamin D 0mcg	0%
Calcium 16mg	1%
Iron 0mg	2%
Potassium 189mg	4%

EGG CUSTARD

Medium

40 minutes

2 Servings

INGREDIENTS:

- 2 eggs
- Pinch of salt
- 6 oz. unsweetened almond milk
- 1 pinch ground cinnamon
- 1 pinch ground nutmeg
- 4 tablespoons maple syrup
- 1 pinch ground cardamom

PREPARATION:

1. Grease 8 small ramekins with butter or cooking spray. Preheat oven to 325 °F.
2. In a bowl, add the eggs and saltand beat well through a hand whisk.
3. In order to get rid of any lumps, pour the mixture through a sieve in a bowl.
4. Add the maple syrup , almond milk and spices and beat until well combined.
5. Transfer the mixture into prepared ramekins and arrange the ramekins into a large baking dish.
6. Add hot water in the baking dish about 2-inch high and pop the dish in the oven.
7. Bake for approximately 30-40 minutes.
8. Remove from the oven and set aside on the cooling rack.
9. Refrigerate to chill before serving.

NUTRITIONAL INFORMATION PER SERVING:

Calories		103
	% Daily Value*	
Total Fat 3.8g		5%
Saturated Fat 1g		5%
Cholesterol 102mg		34%
Sodium 111mg		5%
Total Carbohydrate 14.2g		5%
Dietary Fiber 0.4g		1%
Total Sugars 12g		
Protein 3.8g		
Vitamin D 10mcg		50%
Calcium 115mg		9%
Iron 1mg		5%
Potassium 132mg		3%

WATERMELON SORBET

Very Easy

5 minutes

2 Servings

INGREDIENTS:

- 4 cups cubed (1 inch) watermelon seeds and rind discarded
- 1 tablespoon fresh lemon juice
- ½ cup sugar free maple flavoured syrup

PREPARATION:

1. In a food processor, puree the watermelon chunks. Place 4 cups of the puree in a mixing bowl.
2. Stir in the maple sugar free syrup and lemon juice thoroughly. Churn in the ice cream machine as instructed in the manual.
3. Scoop out and enjoy!

NUTRITIONAL INFORMATION PER SERVING:

Calories	8
	% Daily Value*
Total Fat 0.1g	0%
Saturated Fat 0.1g	0%
Cholesterol 0mg	0%
Sodium 19mg	1%
Total Carbohydrate 2.6g	1%
Dietary Fiber 0g	0%
Total Sugars 0.3g	
Protein 0.1g	
Vitamin D 0mcg	0%
Calcium 1mg	0%
Iron 0mg	0%
Potassium 12mg	0%

ALMOND RICE PUDDING

Medium

120 minutes

2 Servings

INGREDIENTS:

- 1/3 cup white rice
- 1 cup low fat 1% milk
- 4 tablespoons stevia powder
- Cinnamon, to taste
- 4 drops vanilla extract
- 4 drops almond extract
- 4 tablespoons toasted almonds

PREPARATION:

1. Wash and soak rice for 10 min
2. In a medium saucepan, bring the milk to a boil. Add soaked rice in the milk.
3. Reduce to low heat and cover for ½ hour, or until the rice is tender.
4. Eliminate the pan off the heat and stir in the stevia, vanilla, almond essence, and cinnamon.
5. Serve in dessert glasses or bowls and top with toasted almonds.
6. Later refrigerate for up to two hours.
7. Serve chilled and enjoy!

NUTRITIONAL INFORMATION PER SERVING:

Calories	142
	% Daily Value*
Total Fat 2.5g	3%
Saturated Fat 0.7g	4%
Cholesterol 5mg	2%
Sodium 42mg	2%
Total Carbohydrate 23.8g	9%
Dietary Fiber 0.7g	2%
Total Sugars 5g	
Protein 5.4g	
Vitamin D 48mcg	238%
Calcium 124mg	10%
Iron 1mg	6%
Potassium 187mg	4%

COCONUT MACAROONS

Easy

15 minutes

2 Servings

INGREDIENTS:

- ¼ cup low-fat unsweetened coconut, shredded
- ¼ tablespoon coconut flour
- 4 tablespoons pure maple syrup
- ¼ tablespoon olive oil
- ¼ teaspoon organic vanilla extract
- Pinch of salt

PREPARATION:

1. Preheat oven to 350 °F. Line a baking sheet with the silicon sheet or parchment paper.

2. In a food processor, add all the ingredients and pulse until well combined.

3. Put the mixture in the piping bag with the star tip. Pipe out the mixture onto the prepared cookie sheet in a single layer.

4. Bake for approximately 7-10 minutes or until golden brown.

5. Remove from the oven and let them cool for about 1 hour before serving.

NUTRITIONAL INFORMATION PER SERVING:

Calories	171
	% Daily Value*
Total Fat 13.4g	17%
Saturated Fat 9.5g	48%
Cholesterol 0mg	0%
Sodium 12mg	1%
Total Carbohydrate 12.3g	4%
Dietary Fiber 3.9g	14%
Total Sugars 4g	
Protein 1.9g	
Vitamin D 0mcg	0%
Calcium 5mg	0%
Iron 0mg	0%
Potassium 15mg	0%

STUFFED PEARS

Easy

15 minutes

2 Servings

INGREDIENTS:

- ¼ tablespoon unsalted margarine, softened
- ¼ teaspoon olive oil
- 2 pears, halved and cored
- 1/8 cup blue cheese, crumbled
- Crushed walnuts for garnishing (as required)

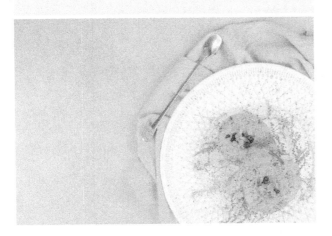

PREPARATION:

1. Grease the grill and preheat
2. In a small bowl, mix together softened margarine and cheese. Set aside.
3. Coat the flesh side of pear halves with oil.
4. Arrange the pear halves onto the grill, skin side downwards.
5. Divide the cheese mixture into the cavity of pear halves evenly.
6. Cook for about 10-15 minutes.
7. Garnish with crushed walnuts.
8. Serve and enjoy!

NUTRITIONAL INFORMATION PER SERVING:

Calories	93
	% Daily Value*
Total Fat 3.4g	4%
Saturated Fat 1.1g	6%
Cholesterol 3mg	1%
Sodium 77mg	3%
Total Carbohydrate 16g	6%
Dietary Fiber 3.2g	12%
Total Sugars 10.2g	
Protein 1.3g	
Vitamin D 0mcg	0%
Calcium 32mg	2%
Iron 0mg	1%
Potassium 133mg	3%

FRUITY SKEWERS

Very Easy

15 minutes

2 Servings

INGREDIENTS:

- 1 cup fresh pineapple, cut into 1-inch pieces
- 1 cup fresh watermelon, pitted and cut into 1 inch pieces.
- Olive oil cooking spray
- 1 tablespoon maple syrup

PREPARATION:

1. Preheat your grill to medium-low heat. Grease the grill with the cooking spray.
2. Thread the fruit pieces onto the pre-soaked wooden skewer.
3. Spray the skewers with cooking spray again and then drizzle with maple syrup.
4. Position the skewers carefully onto the grill and cook for about 10 minutes, flipping occasionally.
5. Serve and enjoy!

NUTRITIONAL INFORMATION PER SERVING:

Calories	90

	% Daily Value*
Total Fat 0.2g	0%
Saturated Fat 0.1g	0%
Cholesterol 0mg	0%
Sodium 3mg	0%
Total Carbohydrate 23.2g	8%
Dietary Fiber 1.5g	5%
Total Sugars 18.7g	
Protein 0.9g	
Vitamin D 0mcg	0%
Calcium 22mg	2%
Iron 1mg	3%
Potassium 195mg	4%

6-WEEK MEAL PLAN

Day 1

Breakfast: Strawberry Ricotta Toast
Lunch: Chicken with Harissa Chickpeas
Snack: Acorn Squash with Apples
Dinner: Chicken and Broccoli Stew

Day 2

Breakfast: Pumpkin Omelet
Lunch: Curried Halibut
Snack: Minted Baby Carrots
Dinner: Rainbow Grain Bowl with Cashew Tahini Sauce

Day 3

Breakfast: Egg Vegetarian Breakfast Salad
Lunch: Oregano Chicken Breast
Snack: Black Bean Patties
Dinner: Turkey and Strawberry Lettuce Wraps

Day 4

Breakfast: Steel-Cut Oats
Lunch: Avocado and Black Bean Eggs
Snack: Eggplant with Toasted Spices
Dinner: Beef Stuffed Tomatoes

Day 5

Breakfast: Overnight Quinoa Pudding
Lunch: Vegan Superfood Grain Bowls
Snack: Stuffed Poblano Peppers
Dinner: Chicken and Green Bean Casserole

Day 6

Breakfast: Summer Skillet Vegetable and Egg
Lunch: Chipotle-Lime Cauliflower Taco Bowls
Snack: Roasted Tomatoes
Dinner: Rosemary Pork Tenderloin

Day 7

Breakfast: Nutritious Egg Bake
Lunch: Spiced Duck Breast
Snack: Holiday Green Bean Casserole
Dinner: Turkey and Strawberry Lettuce Wraps

WEEK 2

Day 1

Breakfast: Yogurt Raspberry Cereal Bowl
Lunch: Mixed Greens with Lentils & Sliced Apple

Snack: Crispy Potato Wedges
Dinner: Garlicky Prime Rib Roast

Day 2

Breakfast: Pumpkin Omelet
Lunch: Chimichurri Noodle Bowls
Snack: Black Sesame Baked Chicken Tenders
Dinner: Lemony Pork Tenderloin

Day 3

Breakfast: Spaghetti Frittata
Lunch: Maple Glazed Turkey Breasts
Snack: Potato Salad
Dinner: Herbed Flank Steak

Day 4

Breakfast: Blueberry Smoothie Bowl
Lunch: Chicken With Cashews and Pineapples
Snack: Vanilla Chia Seed Pudding with Toppings
Dinner: Lamb With Brussels Sprout

Day 5

Breakfast: Raspberry Overnight Muesli
Lunch: Chicken and Spinach Curry
Snack: Mango Banana Soft Serve
Dinner: Lemony Cod

Day 6

Breakfast: Banana and Almond Butter Porridge
Lunch: Mango and Avocado Salad
Snack: Egg Custard
Dinner: Garlicky Haddock

Day 7

Breakfast: Berry-Almond Smoothie Bowl
Lunch: Goat Cheese and Fig Salad
Snack: Banana Berry Ice Cream
Dinner: Chilled Strawberry & Veggie Soup

WEEK 3

Day 1

Breakfast: Breakfast Salad with Egg & Salsa Verde Vinaigrette
Lunch: Orange and Beet Salad
Snack: Strawberry Souffle
Dinner: Peas and Cauliflower Stew

Day 2

Breakfast: Strawberry Ricotta Toast
Lunch: Power Salad with Chickpeas and Tuna
Snack: Fruity Skewers
Dinner: Mahi Mahi and Veggie Soup

Day 3

Breakfast: Oatmeal-Rhubarb Porridge
Lunch: Chicken and VeggieTortellini Salad
Snack: Stuffed Pears
Dinner: Chickpeas and Vegetable Stew

Day 4

Breakfast: Egg Vegetarian Breakfast Salad
Lunch: Lime Egg Vegetable Salad
Snack: Almond Rice Pudding
Dinner: Cucumber Soup

Day 5

Breakfast: Steel-Cut Oats
Lunch: Pickled Beets
Snack: Coconut Macaroons
Dinner: Red Beans Stew

Day 6

Breakfast: Pumpkin Omelet
Lunch: Veggie Hummus Sandwich
Snack: Watermelon Sorbet
Dinner: Kale and Dandelion Greens Soup

Day 7

Breakfast: Summer Skillet Vegetable and Egg
Lunch: Pea & Spinach Carbonara
Snack: Acorn Squash With Apples
Dinner: Lentil, Veggie And Barley Stew

WEEK 4

Day 1

Breakfast: Nutritious Egg Bake
Lunch: Gnocchi Pomodoro
Snack: Minted Baby Carrots
Dinner: Spinach and Beans Soup

Day 2

Breakfast: Yogurt Raspberry Cereal Bowl
Lunch: Stuffed Sweet Potato With Hummus Dressing
Snack: Black Bean Patties
Dinner: Chickpeas and Broccoli Stew

Day 3

Breakfast: Overnight Quinoa Pudding
Lunch: Okra Curry
Snack: Eggplant With Toasted Spices
Dinner: Beef Brisket

Day 4

Breakfast: Spaghetti Frittata
Lunch: Chipotle-Lime Cauliflower Taco Bowls
Snack: Stuffed Poblano Peppers
Dinner: Rainbow Grain Bowl with Cashew Tahini Sauce

Day 5

Breakfast: Blueberry Smoothie Bowl
Lunch: Chickpeas and Vegetable Stew
Snack: Roasted Tomatoes
Dinner: Turkey and Strawberry Lettuce Wraps

Day 6

Breakfast: Raspberry Overnight Muesli
Lunch: Quinoa With Veggies
Snack: Holiday Green Bean Casserole
Dinner: Beef Stuffed Tomatoes

Day 7

Breakfast: Banana and Almond Butter Porridge
Lunch: Orange and Beet Salad
Snack: Crispy Potato Wedges
Dinner: Chicken and Green Bean Casserole

WEEK 5

Day 1

Breakfast Strawberry Ricotta Toast
Lunch: Okra curry
Snack: Black Sesame Baked Chicken Tenders
Dinner: Rosemary Pork Tenderloin

Day 2

Breakfast: Pumpkin Omelet
Lunch: Curried Halibut
Snack: Potato Salad
Dinner: Lentil, Veggie and Barley Stew

Day 3

Breakfast: Egg Vegetarian Breakfast Salad
Lunch: Oregano Chicken Breast
Snack: Mango Banana Soft Serve
Dinner: Garlicky Prime Rib Roast

Day 4

Breakfast: Berrie-Berrie Smoothie
Lunch: Spiced Duck Breast
Snack: Egg Custard
Dinner: Lemony Pork Tenderloin

Day 5

Breakfast: Steel-Cut-Oats
Lunch: Mixed Greens with Lentils & Sliced Apple
Snack: Banana Berry Ice Cream
Dinner: Herbed Flank Steak

Day 6

Breakfast: Beet-Watermelon-Banana Smoothie
Lunch: Chimichurri Noodle Bowls
Snack: Strawberry Souffle
Dinner: Lamb With Brussels Sprout

Day 7

Breakfast: Nutritious Egg Bake
Lunch: Maple Glazed Turkey Breasts
Snack: Fruity Skewers
Dinner: Lemony Cod

WEEK 6

Day 1

Breakfast: Chocolate-Banana Protein Smoothie
Lunch: Pea & Spinach Carbonara
Snack: Stuffed Pears
Dinner: Garlicky Haddock

Day 2

Breakfast: Summer Skillet Vegetable and Egg
Lunch: Gnocchi Pomodoro

Snack: Almond Rice Pudding
Dinner: Peas and Cauliflower Stew

Day 3

Breakfast: Cantaloupe-Watermelon Smoothie
Lunch: Okra Curry
Snack: Coconut Macaroons
Dinner: Chickpeas And Vegetable Stew

Day 4

Breakfast: Overnight Quinoa Pudding
Lunch: Quinoa With Veggies
Snack: Watermelon Sorbet
Dinner: Red Beans Stew

Day 5

Breakfast: Fruit and Yogurt Smoothie
Lunch: Chickpeas With Swiss Chard
Snack: Vanilla Chia Seed Pudding with Toppings
Dinner: Kale and Dandelion Greens Soup

Day 6

Breakfast: Banana and Peanut Butter Porridge
Lunch: Chickpeas And Broccoli Stew
Snack: Minted Baby Carrots
Dinner: Mahi Mahi and Veggie Soup

Day 7

Breakfast: Mango Ginger Smoothie
Lunch: Avocado and Black Bean Eggs
Snack: Black Bean Patties
Dinner: Cucumber Soup

SHOPPING LIST

Poultry, Meat & Seafood

chicken breasts
chicken thighs
chicken tenderloins
ground chicken
cooked chicken
deli turkey
beef tenderloin
prime rib roast
flank steak
lean beef
pork tenderloin
salmon
cod
tilapia

Dairy:

eggs
fat-free milk
skimmed milk
2 % milk
1% milk
butter
margarine
yogurt
sour cream
Mexican blend cheese
cheddar cheese
Monterey Jack cheese
mozzarella cheese
Parmesan cheese
ricotta cheese
feta cheese
goat cheese
blue cheese

Vegetables & Fresh Herbs:

arugula
kale
spinach
watercress
dandelion greens
Swiss chard
mushrooms
asparagus
broccoli
cauliflower
cabbage
potato
sweet potato
okra
eggplant
bell pepper

green beans
green peas
Brussels sprouts
artichokes
acorn squash
butternut squash
beet
carrot
olives
radish
tomato
cucumber
lettuce
salad greens
celery
onion
shallot
fennel
scallion
capers
corn
garlic
ginger
red chilli
poblano pepper
Jalapeno pepper
Serrano pepper
lemon
lime
basil
parsley
coriander
dill
mint
oregano
rosemary
cilantro

Fruit

raspberries
blueberries
strawberries
blackberries
apple
pear
banana
pineapple
mango
watermelon
cantaloupe
orange
avocado

Grains, Nuts & Seeds

oats
chickpeas
black beans
white beans
cannellini beans
lentils
brown rice
white rice
barley
quinoa
almonds
walnuts
hemp seeds
flaxseed
sunflower seeds
mustard seed
sesame seeds
chia seeds

Seasoning & Dried Herbs

salt
black pepper
white pepper
paprika
red chilli powder
cayenne pepper
red pepper flakes
onion powder
garlic powder
cumin
coriander
cinnamon
nutmeg
cardamom
pumpkin spice
za'atar
curry powder
curry paste
Salt Free Garlic
celery seed
bay leaf
thyme
oregano
rosemary
parsley

Extra:

almond milk
coconut milk
Olive oil spray
olive oil

canola oil
rapeseed oil
almond butter
brown sugar
maple syrup
applesauce
honey
molasses
liquid stevia
maple flavoured syrup
mayonnaise
apple cider vinegar
balsamic vinegar
red-wine vinegar
white wine vinegar
soy sauce
vanilla extract
almond extract
tomato sauce
ranch sauce
marinara sauce
hot sauce
salsa
hummus
pesto
Dijon mustard
whole grain mustard
harissa paste
horseradish
whole grain bread
whole-wheat bread
white bread
pita bread
pita round
tortillas
pumpkin puree
tofu
unsweetened coconut
spaghetti
pasta
chicken broth
vegetable broth
kefir
coconut water
dried figs
cheese tortellini
gnocchi
cornstarch
all-purpose flour
coconut flour
breadcrumbs
vegetable bouillon powder

CONCLUSION

The DASH diet is a complete and lifelong approach to healthy eating that is developed to help in treating or preventing high blood pressure (hypertension). The DASH diet encourages you to make changes in your diet and lifestyle by reducing the amount of sodium in your diet and eat foods rich in healthy nutrients that are responsible for lower blood pressure. As part of the DASH diet, you also need to limit your intake of saturated fat, trans fat, cholesterol, added sugars and alcohol. In addition to lowering blood pressure, the DASH diet has been effective in terms of reducing the risk of cardic diseases, stroke and some types of cancer. While the DASH diet isn't a weight loss diet, studies have shown that it can also be helpful to some extent in losing weight and maintain a healthy weight over time. If you want a safe and effective way to improve your overall health, the DASH diet is a great place to start.

"Thank you for purchasing the DASH diet book! I hope you enjoyed it and you found it useful.

I did devote a great deal of time and effort in writing this book, that's why I'm kindly asking you to help me out with sharing this book with as many people as possible.

I would appreciate it if you could leave a review on Amazon. "

DOWNLOAD HERE

YOUR GIFT

Made in the USA
Monee, IL
07 May 2023

33233728R00063